JAN. 07

Digital Evidence in the Courtroom: A Guide for Law Enforcement and Prosecutors

NCJ 211314

David W. Hagy
Deputy Assistant Attorney General,
Office of Justice Programs and Principal Deputy Director,
National Institute of Justice

Opinions or points of view expressed in this document represent a consensus of the authors and do not necessarily represent the official position or policies of the U.S. Department of Justice. The products, manufacturers, and organizations discussed in this document are presented for informational purposes only and do not constitute product approval or endorsement by the U.S. Department of Justice.

This document was prepared under Cooperative Agreement #98–IJ–CX–K003 between the National Institute of Justice and the National Center for Forensic Science.

The National Institute of Justice is a component of the Office of Justice Programs, which also includes the Bureau of Justice Assistance, the Bureau of Justice Statistics, the Office of Juvenile Justice and Delinquency Prevention, and the Office for Victims of Crime.

Foreword

Law enforcement agencies, prosecutors, and judges are overwhelmed by the amount of information required to keep pace with the rapid changes involving the computer and its associated devices and features. Criminals continually alter, revise, or create hardware, software, viruses, and other attacks in an effort to disguise criminal activity and thwart detection. In addition to being familiar with these changes in technology, law enforcement officers and prosecutors also must stay abreast of the latest revisions of applicable laws.

To assist prosecutorial offices and associated law enforcement agencies, the National Institute of Justice (NIJ) has developed a series of guides dealing with digital evidence to address the complete investigation process. This process expands from the crime scene, through analysis, and finally into the courtroom. The guides summarize information from select groups of practitioners who are knowledgeable about the subject matter. These groups are more commonly known as *technical working groups* (TWGs).

This guide is the fourth in this series. The other guides are:

- *Electronic Crime Scene Investigation: A Guide for First Responders,* www.ojp.usdoj.gov/nij/pubs-sum/ 187736.htm.

- *Forensic Examination of Digital Evidence: A Guide for Law Enforcement,* www.ojp.usdoj.gov/nij/pubs-sum/ 199408.htm.

- *Investigations Involving the Internet and Computer Networks,* NCJ 210798, www.ojp.usdoj.gov/nij/pubs-sum/ 210798.htm, publication pending.

The remaining guides in the series will address:

- Using advanced technology to investigate.

- Creating a digital evidence forensic unit.

Because laws continually evolve, the Technical Working Group for Digital Evidence in the Courtroom (TWGDEC) recognizes that its recommendations may not apply in all circumstances. The guide's recommendations are neither mandates nor policy directives, nor do they represent the only correct courses of action. Rather, the recommendations discuss applicable laws combined with a consensus of the experience of the technical working group members to provide valuable insight into the important issues involved with using digital evidence in the courtroom. We hope these recommendations spark discussions about the practices and procedures that are best suited to a jurisdiction's unique environment.

NIJ

NIJ also hopes that these materials will enable more of the Nation's law enforcement personnel and prosecutors to work effectively with digital evidence, maximizing its reliability to the benefit of criminal case prosecutions.

NIJ extends its appreciation to TWGDEC participants for their dedication to the preparation of this guide. Their efforts are particularly commendable given that they participated in TWGDEC while continuing to carry out their duties with their home offices or agencies. Moreover, TWGDEC members had to attend numerous (and

lengthy) guide preparation meetings held at locations far removed from their home offices or agencies. All of us at NIJ appreciate the commitment made by the home offices or agencies of TWGDEC members in making their employees available for this work.

David W. Hagy
Deputy Assistant Attorney General,
Office of Justice Programs and
Principal Deputy Director,
National Institute of Justice

Technical Working Group for Digital Evidence in the Courtroom

TWGDEC was a multidisciplinary group of practitioners and subject-matter experts from across the United States.

Planning panel

Abigail Abraham
Assistant Attorney General
Illinois Attorney General's Office
Chicago, Illinois

Carleton Bryant
Staff Attorney
Knox County Sheriff's Office
Knoxville, Tennessee

Stephen J. Cribari
Defense Attorney
University of Minnesota Law School
Minneapolis, Minnesota

Donald Judges
Ben J. Altheimer Professor of
 Legal Advocacy
University of Arkansas School of Law
Fayetteville, Arkansas

Robert Morgester
Deputy Attorney General
State of California Department of Justice
Office of the Attorney General
Criminal Law Division
Sacramento, California

Ivan Orton
Senior Deputy Prosecuting Attorney
King County Prosecuting Attorney's Office
Fraud Division
Seattle, Washington

Dick Reeve
General Counsel
Second Judicial District
Denver District Attorney's Office
Denver, Colorado

Fred Smith
Attorney
Santa Fe, New Mexico

Richard Salgado
Senior Counsel
U.S. Department of Justice
Criminal Division
Computer Crime and Intellectual
 Property Section
Washington, D.C.

Additional TWGDEC members

Additional members were subsequently incorporated with the planning panel members to create the full technical working group. The individuals listed below worked together with the planning panel to formulate this guide.

Steven Beltz
Washington State Patrol
Olympia, Washington

Robert Beitler
Florida Department of Law Enforcement
Computer Evidence Recovery
Tallahassee Regional Operations Center
Tallahassee, Florida

John Boesman
Prince George's County Police Department
Palmer Park, Maryland

Don Buchwald
Project Engineer
Aerospace Corporation
Los Angeles, California

Don Colcolough
AOL Time Warner, Inc.
Dulles, Virginia

Kevin Comerford
Erie County Police Services
Buffalo, New York

William Crane
Assistant Director
Computer Crime Section
National White Collar Crime Center
Fairmont, West Virginia

Jeff Dort
Deputy District Attorney
Internet Crimes Against Children
  Task Force
San Diego District Attorney's Office
Family Protection Division
San Diego, California

Donald Flynn, Jr.
Attorney Advisor
Cyber Crime Center
U.S. Department of Defense
Washington, D.C.

William Fulton
Texas Department of Public Safety
Special Crimes Services
San Antonio, Texas

Mary Horvath
Federal Bureau of Investigation
Washington, D.C.

Roland Lascola
Federal Bureau of Investigation
Washington, D.C.

Barry Leese
Detective Sergeant, Ret.
Maryland State Police
Computer Crimes Unit
Columbia, Maryland

Stacey Levine
Criminal Division
Computer Crime and Intellectual
  Property Section
U.S. Department of Justice
Washington, D.C.

Jim May
Prince George's County Police Department
Palmer Park, Maryland

Justin Price
Florida Department of Law Enforcement
Computer Evidence Recovery
Tampa, Florida

Dan Purcell
Investigator
Seminole County Sheriff's Office
Economic Crimes Unit/Computer
  Forensics
Sanford, Florida

Chris Romolo
United States Secret Service
Washington, D.C.

Joseph Schwerha, IV
Assistant District Attorney
Office of the District Attorney
Washington, Pennsylvania

Carl Selavka
National Institute of Justice
U.S. Department of Justice
Washington, D.C.

John A. Sgromolo
Director of Investigations and Training
LC Technology International
Clearwater, Florida

Todd Shipley
Detective
Reno Police Department
Computer Crimes Unit
Reno, Nevada

Rebecca Springer
Assistant Statewide Prosecutor
Florida Office of Statewide Prosecution
Central Florida Bureau
Orlando, Florida

Scott Stein
Cybercrimes Unit
Office of the U.S. Attorney for the Eastern
  District of Virginia
Alexandria, Virginia

Chris Stippich
Digital Intelligence, Inc.
Waukesha, Wisconsin

Mike Swangler
United States Secret Service
Washington, D.C.

Jeanette Supera
Senior Investigator
Office of the Attorney General
State of Nevada
Carson City, Nevada

Wayne Williams
Williams Enterprises
Hyattsville, Maryland

Terry Willis
Computer Crime Unit Supervisor
Los Angeles Police Department
Los Angeles, California

Facilitators

John Bardakjy
Project Manager
National Center for Forensic Science
Orlando, Florida

Dale Heideman
Deputy Director
National Center for Forensic Science
Orlando, Florida

Anjali Swienton
ACS Defense, Inc.
Contracted to the National Institute
  of Justice
U.S. Department of Justice
Washington, D.C.
and
President and CEO
SciLawForensics, Ltd.
Germantown, Maryland

Carrie Whitcomb
Director
National Center for Forensic Science
Orlando, Florida

Amon Young
Program Manager
National Institute of Justice
U.S. Department of Justice
Washington, D.C.

Contents

Introduction

*Note: Terms that appear in the glossary appear in **bold italics** upon their first appearance in this guide.*

The rapid, widespread adoption of new technology often outpaces society's development of a shared ethic governing its use and the ability of legal systems to deal with it. The handling of **digital evidence** is a perfect example.

Although computers have existed for more than 60 years, it has been only since the late 1980s, as computers have proliferated in businesses, homes, and government agencies, that digital evidence has been used to solve crimes and prosecute offenders.

For example, for years, evidence in child pornography cases was found in magazines and consisted of traditional photographs. During the mid-1990s, the Internet changed that. Now it is rare to find a child pornography case that involves anything other than digital images and printouts of those images.

Once the province of "computer crime" cases such as hacking, digital evidence is now found in every crime category. Too often, though, law enforcement agencies and the judiciary are ill-prepared to deal with the issues created by the increasing use of this evidence.

Some judges, attorneys, and jurors may harbor doubts about the reliability and significance of digital evidence. To prevent misunderstandings at trial, concepts must be explained in simple terms with carefully selected analogies and visual aids.

Prosecutors should not assume that investigators understand how to avoid creating confusion at trial. Technically sophisticated investigators or examiners should not assume that prosecutors fully grasp the problems encountered in recovering and analyzing the evidence. Prosecutors, investigators, and examiners should share their knowledge of technical problems and discuss strategies.

Addressed to law enforcement and prosecutors, this report is subject to several important limitations and, therefore, is only a guide. First, it identifies and briefly addresses some of the key issues related to digital evidence. More extensive treatment can be found in resources referenced throughout the guide and in appendix A. Second, many issues discussed are subject to laws that vary from jurisdiction to jurisdiction. Third, the technology and law in this area are rapidly evolving. Finally, this guide does not address the acquisition of digital evidence from outside the United States (criminal investigators and prosecutors should consult the Office of International Affairs, U.S. Department of Justice, 202–514–0000).

I. Background

The collection of digital evidence in criminal cases is governed at the Federal and State levels by numerous constitutional and statutory provisions, including statutes that regulate the communications and computer industries and that directly govern the gathering and use of digital evidence. Court decisions and procedural rules also need to be considered.

This chapter discusses several Federal statutes that govern access to and disclosure of certain types of information deemed deserving of special treatment by Congress: the Electronic Communications Privacy Act (which includes the Wiretap Act, the Pen Register and Trap and Trace Statute, and the Stored Wire and Electronic Communications Act) and the Privacy Protection Act. Also reviewed are principles applicable under the Fourth Amendment to the U.S. Constitution. Investigators, examiners, and prosecutors should be familiar with these statutes because their breach may result in evidentiary challenge or civil suit. (Other Federal provisions and State laws are beyond the scope of this guide.)

NOTE: A comprehensive analysis of Federal search and seizure issues can be found in *Searching and Seizing Computers and Obtaining Electronic Evidence in Criminal Investigations* (www.cybercrime.gov/s&smanual2002.htm).

II. Wiretap Act

The Wiretap Act (18 U.S.C. § 2510 et seq.) focuses on the interception of the content of communications while they are in transit. Examples of such interceptions include wiretapping a telephone, placing a listening device or "bug" in a room to pick up conversations, and installing *"sniffer"* software that captures a hacker's instant messages. The Wiretap Act also governs the disclosure of intercepted communications.

The Wiretap Act generally and broadly prohibits anyone in the United States from intercepting the contents of wire, oral, or electronic communications. As a basic rule, the Wiretap Act prohibits anyone who is not a participating party to a private communication from intercepting the communication between or among the participating parties using an "electronic, mechanical, or other device," unless one of several statutory exceptions applies.

One exception is the issuance of an order by a court of competent jurisdiction that authorizes interception. The requirements to obtain such an order are substantial.

Violation of the Wiretap Act can lead to criminal and civil liability. In the case of wire and oral communications, a violation by government officials may result in the suppression of evidence. To ensure compliance, an initial determination should be made about whether:

■ The communication to be monitored is one of the protected communications defined in the statute.

■ The proposed surveillance constitutes an "interception" of the communication.

If both conditions are present, an evaluation should be conducted to determine whether a statutory exception applies that permits the interception.

> **NOTE:** Some States have versions of the Wiretap Act that are more restrictive than the Federal act. The Federal act does *not* preempt State laws unless Federal officers are conducting the investigation. State and local law enforcement must comply with any such State act, even if no violation of the Federal Wiretap Act occurs.

> In *U.S.* v. *Councilman,* 418 F.3d 67 (1st Cir. 2005)(en banc), involving the use of delivery software to copy e-mails while those messages existed in the provider's RAM or hard drive pending delivery to the customer, the court ruled that "the term 'electronic communication' includes transient electronic storage that is intrinsic to the communication process, and hence that interception of an e-mail in such storage is an offense under the Wiretap Act." *Id.* at 85.

III. Pen/Trap statute

The Pen Register and Trap and Trace Statute (18 U.S.C. § 3121 et seq.), known as the *Pen/Trap statute,* governs the real-time acquisition of dialing, routing, addressing, and signaling information relating to communications. Unlike the Wiretap Act, the Pen/Trap statute does not cover acquisition of the content of communications. Rather, it covers the information about communications. The term "pen register" refers to a device that records outgoing connection information. A "trap and trace" device records incoming connection information. For example, a pen register captures the telephone number dialed by an individual under surveillance, while a trap-and-trace device captures the telephone number of the party who is calling the individual under surveillance.

The Pen/Trap statute applies to telephone and Internet communications. For example, every e-mail communication contains "to" and "from" information. A pen/trap device captures such information in real time.

The statute generally forbids the nonconsensual real-time acquisition of noncontent information by any person about a wire or electronic communication unless a statutory exception applies. When no exception to this prohibition applies, law enforcement must obtain a pen/trap order from the court before acquiring noncontent information covered by the statute.

> **NOTE:** Examples of requests for Federal pen/trap orders may be found at *Searching and Seizing Computers and Obtaining Electronic Evidence in Criminal Investigations* (www.cybercrime.gov/s&smanual2002.htm). Some States have versions of the Pen/Trap statute that are more restrictive than the Federal act. The Federal act does *not* preempt these laws unless Federal **agents** conduct the investigation. State and local law enforcement must comply with any such State act, even if no violation of the Federal Pen/Trap statute occurs.

IV. Stored communications provisions of the Electronic Communications Privacy Act

The stored communications chapter of the Electronic Communications Privacy Act (**ECPA**) (18 U.S.C. § 2701 et seq.) provides privacy protections to customers of and subscribers to certain communications services providers. This statute protects records held (e.g., billing) as well as files stored (e.g., e-mail, uploaded files) by providers for customers and subscribers. Depending on the type of provider, ECPA may dictate what type of legal process is necessary to compel a provider to disclose specific types of customer and subscriber information to law enforcement. ECPA also limits what a provider may and may not voluntarily disclose to others, including Federal, State, or local governments. (For a quick-reference guide to ECPA's disclosure rules, see appendix B.)

ECPA applies when law enforcement seeks to obtain records about a customer or subscriber from a communications services provider (e.g., an **Internet service provider** (**ISP**) or cellular phone provider). For example, ECPA may apply when law enforcement seeks to obtain copies of a customer's e-mails from an ISP. ECPA does not apply when law enforcement seeks to obtain the same e-mails from the customer's computer.

Under ECPA, the production of some information may be compelled by subpoena, some by court order under section 2703(d) (discussed below), and some by search warrant. Generally speaking, the more sensitive the information (from basic subscriber information to transactional information to content of certain kinds of stored communications), the higher the level of legal process required to compel disclosure (from subpoena to court order under 2703(d) to search warrant).

As the level of government process escalates from subpoena to 2703(d) order to search warrant, the information available under the less exacting standard is included at the higher level (e.g., a search warrant grants access to basic subscriber information, transactional information, and content of stored communications).

> **NOTE:** Because providers may use different terms to describe the types of data they hold, it is advisable to consult with each provider on its preferred language to make obtaining the information as easy as possible.

A. Subpoena: subscriber and session information

Under ECPA, law enforcement may use a subpoena to compel a service provider to disclose the following information about the identity of a customer or subscriber, that person's relationship with the service provider, and basic session connection records:

1. Name.

2. Address.

3. Local and long distance telephone connection records, or records of session times and durations.

4. Length of service (including start date) and types of service used.

5. Telephone or instrument number or other subscriber number or identity, including any temporarily assigned **network** address.

6. The means and source of payment for such service (including credit card and bank account numbers).

Notably, this list does not include extensive transaction-related records, such as logging information that reveals the e-mail addresses of persons with whom a customer corresponded during prior sessions, or "**buddy lists**."

B. Court order under 2703(d): other noncontent subscriber and session information

Law enforcement must obtain a court order under 18 U.S.C. § 2703(d) to compel a provider to disclose more detailed records about a customer's or subscriber's use of services, such as the following:

1. Account activity logs that reflect what Internet protocol (IP) addresses the subscriber visited over time.

2. Addresses of others from and to whom the subscriber exchanged e-mail.

3. Buddy lists.

Law enforcement can also use a 2703(d) order to compel a cellular telephone service provider to turn over, in real time, records showing the cell-site location information for calls made from a subscriber's cellular phone. These records provide more information about a subscriber's use of the system than those available by subpoena, but they do not include the content of the communications.

A Federal magistrate or district court with jurisdiction over the offense under investigation may issue a 2703(d) order. State court judges authorized by the law of the State to enter orders authorizing the use of a pen/trap device may also issue 2703(d) orders. The application must offer "specific and articulable facts showing that there are reasonable grounds to believe that . . . the records or other information sought are relevant and material to an ongoing criminal investigation."

NOTE: In general, ECPA provides more privacy protection for the contents of communications and files stored with a provider than for records detailing the use of a service or a subscriber's identity. Refer to *Searching and Seizing Computers and Obtaining Electronic Evidence in Criminal Investigations* (www.cybercrime.gov/ s&smanual2002.htm) for examples of applications for an order under 2703(d).

C. Content of stored communications

ECPA distinguishes between communications in storage that have already been retrieved by the customer or subscriber and those that have not. In addition, the act distinguishes between retrieved communications that are held by a private provider (e.g., an employer who offers e-mail services to employees and contractors only) and those held by a provider that offers its services to the public generally.

1. Subpoena: retrieved communications held by private provider.

   ECPA applies only to stored communications that a customer or subscriber has retrieved but left on a public service provider's **server**, if the service provider offers those services to the public (see section IV.C.2). If a provider does not offer such services to the public, no constraints are imposed by ECPA on the provider's right to disclose such information voluntarily.

   ECPA does not require any heightened or particular legal process to compel disclosure of such records. For example, ECPA does not apply to a government request to compel an employer to produce the retrieved e-mail of a particular employee if the employer offers e-mail services and accounts to its employees but not to the public generally. Where ECPA does not apply, such information may be available through traditional legal processes.

NOTE: ECPA may apply if the e-mail being sought resides on the employer's server and has not yet been retrieved by the employee. In this instance, the rules discussed under section IV.C.3 (below) apply.

2. Subpoena or 2703(d), with notice: retrieved communications, unretrieved communications older than 180 days, and other files stored with a public provider.

   ECPA applies to stored communications that a customer or subscriber has retrieved but left on the server of a communications services provider if the provider offers those services to the public. Such communications include text files, pictures, and programs that a customer may have stored on the public provider's system. Under the statute, such a provider is considered a "remote computing service" and is not permitted to disclose voluntarily such content to the government.

   Law enforcement may use either a subpoena or a 2703(d) court order to compel a public service provider to disclose the contents of stored communications retrieved by a customer or subscriber. In either case, however, law enforcement *must give prior notice of the request to the customer or subscriber.*

Another ECPA provision allows law enforcement to delay giving notice to the customer or subscriber when it would jeopardize a pending investigation or endanger the life or physical safety of an individual. If using a subpoena to compel the disclosure of stored, retrieved communications from a public service provider, law enforcement may seek to delay notice for 90 days "upon the execution of a written certification of a supervisory agent that there is reason to believe that notification of the existence of the subpoena may have an adverse result." If using a 2703(d) order, law enforcement may seek permission from the court to delay notice as part of the application for the order.

At the end of the delayed notice period, law enforcement must send a copy of the request or process to the customer or subscriber, along with a letter explaining the delay.

Law enforcement may also use a subpoena or a 2703(d) order with prior notice to compel a service provider to disclose communications that are unretrieved but have been on the server more than 180 days. As a practical matter, most providers will not allow unretrieved messages to stay on a server unaccessed for such a long period.

If law enforcement is using a search warrant or seeking noncontent information, no notice is required.

NOTE: In *Theofel* v. *Farey-Jones*, 359 F.3d 1066 (9th Cir. 2004), the court ruled that copies of e-mails remaining on an ISP's server after delivery to the customer receive the same protection under ECPA as e-mails stored pending delivery.

---

3. Search warrant: unretrieved communications.

Unretrieved communications, including voice mail,* held by a provider for up to 180 days have the highest level of protection available under ECPA. ECPA covers such communications whether the service provider is private or public. The service provider is generally not permitted to voluntarily disclose unretrieved communications to the government.

For example, under ECPA an e-mail sent to a customer is considered unretrieved if it resides on the server of the customer's provider (i.e., an ISP or the customer's employer), but the customer has not yet logged on and accessed the message. Once the customer accesses the e-mail (but a copy remains on the server of the provider), the e-mail is deemed retrieved. (Refer to chapter 1, section IV.C.1, of this guide for more details about retrieved communications.)

---

* The USA PATRIOT Improvement and Reauthorization Act of 2005 (P.L. 109–177) made permanent section 209 of the USA PATRIOT Act, which allows retrieval of voice mail with a search warrant rather than an intercept order.

Law enforcement may seek a search warrant, such as a warrant provided by 2703(a), to compel a service provider to produce unretrieved communications in storage. No prior notice to the customer or subscriber is required.

> NOTE: Nonpublic providers may voluntarily disclose subscriber and session information, transactional information, and stored communications and files to the government and others without violating ECPA. Under certain circumstances, public providers may also voluntarily disclose information without violating ECPA. Some States may have applicable laws that are more restrictive than the Federal act. The Federal act does *not* preempt these laws unless Federal agents are conducting the investigation. State and local law enforcement must comply with any such State act, even if no violation of the Federal statute occurs.

D. Remedy: civil damages

Civil damages are the exclusive remedy for nonconstitutional violations of ECPA. Evidence seized in violation of ECPA alone should not be suppressed.

V. Privacy Protection Act

The Privacy Protection Act (PPA) (42 U.S.C. § 2000aa et seq.) limits law enforcement's use of a search warrant to search for or seize certain materials possessed for the purpose of public dissemination. The protected materials may be either "work products" (i.e., materials created by the author or publisher) or "documentary materials" (i.e., any materials that document or support the work product).

For example, a person who is creating an online newsletter may possess interview notes that could be considered "documentary materials"; the text of the newsletter to be published could be considered a "work product."

If the material is covered by PPA, law enforcement cannot use a search warrant to obtain it.

PPA's prohibition on the use of a search warrant may *not* apply when:

- Materials searched for or seized are "fruits" or instrumentalities of the crime or are contraband.

- There is reason to believe that the immediate seizure of such materials is necessary to prevent death or serious bodily injury.

- There is probable cause to believe that the person possessing the materials has committed or is committing a criminal offense to which the materials relate. (Except for the possession of child pornography and certain government information, this exception does not apply where the mere possession of the materials constitutes the offense.)

If evidence of a crime is commingled on a computer with PPA-protected materials, issues concerning proper scope and execution of a search warrant will arise. Recent cases indicate that the courts are limiting the scope of PPA protection to people who are not suspected of committing a crime. Evidence seized in violation of PPA alone will not be suppressed.

Civil damages are the exclusive remedy for violation of PPA.

NOTE: For further information on the Privacy Protection Act, see *Searching and Seizing Computers and Obtaining Electronic Evidence in Criminal Investigations* (www.cybercrime.gov/s&smanual2002.htm).

VI. Constitutional issues

Searches for digital evidence, like searches for other forms of evidence, are subject to the constraints of Federal and State constitutional search and seizure laws and court rules. Traditional Fourth Amendment principles, such as those governing closed containers, apply to digital evidence.

A. Applying the Fourth Amendment

The Fourth Amendment protects individuals from unreasonable searches and seizures. Two primary requirements are necessary for Fourth Amendment protections to apply:

- Is government action involved?

- Does the person affected have a reasonable expectation of privacy in the place to be searched or thing to be seized?

1. Government action.

   In most circumstances, government action is implicated when a government official conducts a search. Generally speaking, the Fourth Amendment's limitations do not apply to searches by private parties unless those searches are conducted at the direction of the government. Private parties who independently acquire evidence of a crime may turn it over to law enforcement. (Law enforcement may replicate a private search, but may not exceed the scope of that search without a warrant or exception to the warrant requirement.)

   For example, if an employee discovers contraband files on a computer that is being repaired in a shop, the employee's subsequent release of information to law enforcement does not violate the Fourth Amendment. In such a case, law enforcement may examine anything that the employee observed.

2. Reasonable expectation of privacy.

   The Fourth Amendment applies when the searched party has an actual expectation of privacy in the place to be searched or thing to be seized, and then only if it is an

expectation that society is prepared to recognize as reasonable. Some courts treat a computer as a "closed container" for Fourth Amendment purposes. In some jurisdictions, looking at a computer's subdirectories and files is akin to opening a closed container.

B. Satisfying Fourth Amendment requirements

If the Fourth Amendment is implicated in the search at issue, then generally law enforcement must obtain a warrant unless an exception to the warrant requirement applies.

1. Warrantless searches.

   There are several well-recognized exceptions to securing a warrant. Although the following is not an exhaustive list, the examples provide an idea of how the common exceptions apply to the search and seizure of digital evidence.

   a. Consent.

      Consent is a valuable tool for an investigator. It can come from many sources, including a log-in banner, terms-of-use agreement, or company policy. Some considerations include:

      (1) Like a shared apartment, a computer can have multiple users. Consent by one user is always sufficient to authorize a search of that person's private area of the computer, and in most instances is sufficient to authorize a search of the common areas as well. Additional consent may be needed if an investigator encounters password-protected files. Also, a parent in most cases can consent to a search of a minor child's computer.

      (2) Consent can be limited by subject matter, duration, and other parameters. Consent can be withdrawn at any time (see appendix C for a sample consent form).

      (3) The general rule is that a private-sector employer can consent to a search of an employee's workplace computer. The rules are more complicated when the employer is the government.

      > NOTE: For further information on consent rules, refer to *Searching and Seizing Computers and Obtaining Electronic Evidence in Criminal Investigations* (www.cybercrime.gov/s&smanual2002.htm).

   b. Exigent circumstances.

      To prevent the destruction of evidence, law enforcement can seize an electronic storage device. In certain cases in which there is an immediate danger of losing data, law enforcement may perform a limited search to preserve the data in its current state. Once the exigent circumstances end, so does the exception.

c. Search incident to arrest.

The need to protect the safety of law enforcement or to preserve evidence can justify a full search of an arrestee and a limited search of the arrest scene. This search incident to arrest can include a search of an electronic storage device, such as a cell phone or pager, held by the subject.

NOTE: Although a search incident to arrest may allow the search of electronic storage devices found on the suspect, the arresting law enforcement officer should take care to maintain the integrity of the evidence.

d. Inventory search.

The inventory search exception is intended to protect the property of a person in custody and guard against claims of damage or loss. This exception is untested in the courts, so it is uncertain whether the inventory search exception will allow law enforcement to access digital evidence without a warrant.

e. Plain view doctrine.

The *plain view* doctrine may apply in some instances to the search for and seizure of **electronic evidence**. For plain view to apply, law enforcement must legitimately be in the position to observe evidence, the incriminating character of which must be immediately apparent. Law enforcement officials should exercise caution when relying on the plain view doctrine in connection with digital media, as rules concerning the application of the doctrine vary among jurisdictions.

2. Searches and seizures pursuant to warrants.

If the Fourth Amendment is implicated in a search and none of the search warrant exceptions applies, law enforcement should obtain a search warrant. Generally, the same warrant rules apply when preparing and executing a search warrant for digital evidence as in other investigations. Law enforcement should consider the following when preparing and executing a search warrant for electronic evidence:

a. Describing property.

If the evidence sought is the computer itself (and the hardware is an instrumentality, a fruit of the crime, or contraband), then the warrant should describe the computer as the target of the search.

If the evidence sought is information that may be stored on digital media, then the warrant should describe what that evidence is and request the authority to seize it in whatever form (including digital) it may be stored. This includes requesting authority to search for evidence of ownership and control of the relevant data on the media. Avoid drafting warrants that would unnecessarily restrict the scope of the search.

NOTE: For sample language, see *Searching and Seizing Computers and Obtaining Electronic Evidence in Criminal Investigations* (www.cybercrime.gov/ s&smanual2002.htm).

b. Conducting a search.

In some cases, a search of an electronic storage device can require significant technical knowledge and should be conducted by appropriate personnel who are supplied with a copy of the search warrant to ensure that the search is within its scope.

In the course of conducting a search, law enforcement may discover passwords and keys that could facilitate access to the system and data. Law enforcement may also find evidence of a crime that is outside the scope of the search warrant. In such an event, consider securing another warrant to expand the scope of the search.

See chapter 2 for more indepth discussion.

NOTE: For a discussion of some of the issues concerning evidence collection, see *Electronic Crime Scene Investigation: A Guide for **First Responders*** (www.ojp.usdoj.gov/nij/pubs-sum/187736.htm).

c. Reasonable accommodations.

In some cases, it might be impractical to search the device onsite. If a device is to be searched offsite, law enforcement should consider adding language to the warrant affidavit that justifies its removal.

If a device is removed for an off-scene search, the search should be completed in a timely manner. Law enforcement may consider returning copies of noncontraband seized data, even if they are commingled with evidence of a crime, to accommodate a reasonable request from suspects or third parties.

See chapter 2 for more indepth discussion.

VII. Privileged or proprietary information

In some instances, law enforcement may have reason to believe that the place to be searched will contain information that is considered "privileged" under statute or common law (e.g., the office of a lawyer, health professional, or member of the clergy). Before drafting a warrant and conducting the search, law enforcement should take care to identify and comply with the legal limitations that the jurisdiction may impose. Law enforcement also may wish to:

- Consider the use of **taint teams** (also known as **privilege teams**), **special masters**, or another process, as approved by the court.

- Consider in advance whether the media to be seized contain privileged or proprietary information.

- Consider obtaining a stipulation before seizing information from the target to avoid confiscating potentially privileged or proprietary information. (See appendix D, "Stipulation Regarding Evidence Returned to the Defendant," for an example.)

- To avoid tainting the acquisition of evidence, ensure that the prosecution team addresses the issue of privileged or proprietary information when drafting the search warrant.

VIII. Obtaining out-of-State records

A. The problem

Often the ISP from which State or local law enforcement wishes to obtain records is located outside their State. Of course, for out-of-State entities with a physical presence in the seeking State, service of process on an appropriate local business representative or on a designated agent may be sufficient to acquire jurisdiction over the records. For out-of-State entities who have no physical presence in a State but who are registered as a foreign (out-of-State) business entity or corporation, service on a designated agent may be sufficient.

In other circumstances, the need to obtain records from out-of-State third-party record-holders presents two problems:

1. The seeking State's law may limit the jurisdictional reach of compulsory process, such as subpoenas, orders under 18 U.S.C. 2703(d) ("D-orders"), or search warrants, to its own territorial jurisdiction. Even if there is no explicit law limiting the jurisdictional scope, judges may refuse to issue extraterritorial process.

2. The out-of-State recordholders may refuse to honor process issued from outside the State in which the records are located. Only a few States explicitly require entities located within their territorial jurisdiction to comply with the out-of-State process as if it had been issued in the State. Thus, even if process can be obtained, the out-of-State entity often believes (sometimes correctly) that it is under no legal obligation to comply. Usually this refusal to comply is based on a fear of liability under the ECPA (or, in the case of banks, Federal and State bank privacy laws), i.e., if the warrant is not legally binding then it cannot protect a company from liability for disclosure. In other instances, however, this appears to be more of a "we don't have to so we're not going to" attitude.

NOTE: A few States do require entities within their State to comply with the out-of-State process as if it had been issued in State.

B. Current options

In the following discussion of current options for obtaining out-of-State records, keep in mind that even if the use of State procedures to obtain out-of-State records is held invalid, there is no suppression remedy under the U.S. Constitution. The only Federal remedy for improperly seized ISP records is statutory under the ECPA, which does not include a suppression remedy for nonconstitutional violations. State constitutional or statutory provisions, however, may provide a State suppression remedy. Current options are discussed below.

1. Persuade the court.

   Unless the seeking State has specific prohibitions against extraterritorial process, the prosecution may attempt to persuade the court to issue such process on the grounds that:

   a. There is no specific prohibition on the issuance of such process.

   b. There may be State case law recognizing that search warrants can legitimately be served like a subpoena.

   c. If the warrant is viewed like a subpoena supported by probable cause, then the issue of whether a domestic (in-State) court can direct peace officers of another State does not arise as the foreign State's peace officers are not involved.

   d. As some commentators have argued, local courts have jurisdiction to compel production of evidence located in other States at least to the same extent they have jurisdiction to compel the attendance to trial of out-of-State witnesses.

   The justification for a court's authority to issue warrants for out-of-State records is that the judge is ordering law enforcement to execute the search by faxing or otherwise serving the warrant from the home State on the out-of-State recordholder.

2. Persuade the recordholder.

   Officers from the seeking State who have a validly issued extraterritorial search warrant may be able to persuade an otherwise reluctant out-of-State recordholder to comply. By using some of the same arguments law enforcement used to convince the judge to issue the warrant, law enforcement can attempt to convince the recordholder that (a) the ECPA requires the production of records in response to a lawful search warrant, and (b) the officer has a lawful search warrant. Officers may explain that an entity with a good-faith reliance on process enjoys a complete defense to any civil or criminal action brought under ECPA.

3. Consider other options.

   If a presiding judge refuses to issue an extraterritorial search warrant or a recipient refuses to comply, law enforcement will have to consider other options, such as:

a. Trial subpoena (if charges have been filed).

b. Grand jury or other investigative subpoena (prefiling), which does not have territorial limitations.

c. Trial or grand jury subpoena, used together with the Uniform Act to Secure the Attendance of Witnesses From Without a State in Criminal Proceedings (hereafter referred to as "the Uniform Act").

A subpoena may succeed when a warrant does not. Most States do not have laws directly limiting the jurisdictional reach of subpoenas (and in the case of the Uniform Act, States that have adopted the Act have implicitly or explicitly asserted jurisdiction to issue subpoenas [including subpoenae duces tecum] to residents of other States).

The successful use of a subpoena, however, depends on whether the records sought are obtainable under the ECPA by subpoena as opposed to D-order or search warrant.

The first two subpoenas (trial subpoena or grand jury subpoena) may present the same problem as a search warrant does—the recipient may choose not to comply.

The Uniform Act offers the advantage of the full force of law. Judges have authority to issue subpoenas under the Act, and the recipient must comply. The procedure, however, is cumbersome and time consuming and can only be used to obtain documents when a court hearing is scheduled.

4. "Domesticate" the warrant.

An effective method of getting a valid, enforceable warrant is to prepare an affidavit, send it to law enforcement in the foreign State, and request that that State's law enforcement use the seeking State's affidavit to obtain its own search warrant.

There are several disadvantages to using this process:

■ It depends on cooperation from law enforcement in the foreign State.

■ It is cumbersome, in that it requires two law enforcement agencies to be involved.

■ The seeking State is dependent upon the foreign law enforcement agency's agreement that probable cause for a search exists.

C. Proposed Federal legislation

Federal legislation has been proposed that would require each State to give full faith and credit to the production orders issued by State courts in criminal cases. If enacted, this legislation could be a starting point for a nationwide system allowing States to issue fully enforceable production orders to recordholders in other States. To obtain information on this and other legislation, go to www.ecpi-us.org.

In the meantime, some States have adopted the approach of requiring out-of-State companies registered in State to designate an in-State agent to accept service of in-State process, and requiring companies incorporated in State to accept out-of-State process as if it were issued in State.

Chapter 2. Integrity, Discovery, and Disclosure of Digital Evidence

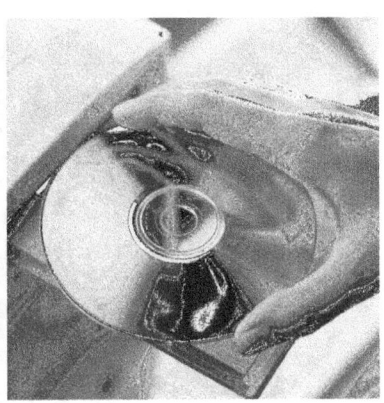

Maintaining the integrity of digital evidence throughout the process of examination presents different problems from those encountered when handling traditional physical or documentary evidence. Some common problems are exacerbated by the complexity of networked computers. This guide does not address the unique issues that may result from networked environments, focusing rather on selected issues of maintaining the integrity of information taken from stand-alone electronic media (see appendix A for a listing of sources related to network forensics).

This guide assumes that the seized media contain relevant information and that the forensic procedures used to examine that media have not altered the evidence since it was seized. After seizure, ensuring that the traditional chain of custody remains unbroken is necessary but not sufficient to establish the authenticity of the data or evidence obtained from the forensic examination. In addition to the traditional chain of custody, auxiliary precautions may be required for handling digital evidence.

This guide also assumes that tools recognized by the forensic community are used in the recovery of digital evidence from the source ***electronic device*** or media. Because the process used to acquire the data is itself electronic, both the evidence and the process may be subject to legal challenges. Additional expertise may be required to authenticate the machine, applications, and forensic tools. Chapter 3 discusses these issues in more depth.

> **NOTE:** See NIJ's Computer Forensic Tool Testing Project Web site (www.ojp.usdoj.gov/nij/topics/ecrime/cftt.htm) for results of tests designed to ensure the accuracy of computer forensic tools.

I. Preliminary inquiries

In some cases, digital evidence may have been intentionally or unwittingly altered before it was secured by law enforcement. This is particularly likely in crimes discovered and investigated by a victim before the victim involves law enforcement. Evidence turned over to the prosecuting authorities for examination ultimately may not be useful without establishing the authenticity and chain of custody of the evidence.

> **NOTE:** When evaluating the evidence, refer to the jurisdiction's statutes to identify possible crimes, including noncomputer crimes that might be involved. Make a checklist of the elements that must be proved if cases go to trial. Consult other NIJ guides in this series for sample questions for specific kinds of computer-involved crimes (see Foreword).

Sample questions that may need to be asked of the person or people providing the evidence include the following:

- What evidence indicates that a crime was committed by an unknown intruder or that a known user exceeded his or her authorized access to the machines or data?

- What is the chronology of the access to or changes in the data?

- What are the estimated damages?

- Who may be responsible for the incident?

- Why is the person (or people) suspected?

- What is the impact on the business?

- Are computers and systems required to run the business?

- When did the incident first occur?

- When was the incident first discovered?

- Who has investigated the incident?

- What actions have been taken to identify, collect, preserve, or analyze the data and the devices involved?

These preliminary inquiries will help the prosecutor provide the necessary foundation for the evidence offered in the case. Once the information is admitted into evidence, the focus will turn to the weight the evidence is accorded. Admissibility is only the first hurdle: Credibility and persuasiveness of the evidence must still be assessed by the *trier of fact*.

II. Integrity of data

Both for purposes of admissibility and persuasive value of digital evidence, the prosecutor must show in court that the information obtained from the media is a true and accurate representation of the data originally contained in the media, irrespective of whether the acquisition was done entirely by law enforcement or in part or entirely by a civilian witness or victim.

A. Chain of custody

Two chains of custody are involved: the physical item itself and its associated data. Be aware that the chain-of-custody issues regarding data are additional to the chain-of-custody issues regarding the physical item.

Know the accreditation standards and laboratory policies, procedures, or other guidelines, if any, regarding chain of custody, both generally and for electronic evidence specifically. Determine whether they have been followed or whether a deviation has occurred. Understand the effect that all deviations may have on the case and be prepared to explain them. Also be aware that the policies, procedures, or other guidelines should

be dynamic. The prosecution team must know which practices were applicable at the time the examination was conducted.

B. Acquisition and examination processes

Employees (e.g., information technology staff, security) of a victimized company should be asked a series of questions pertaining to the preliminary handling of any digital evidence they have provided or will provide to law enforcement. Sufficient time should be allowed to collect and document answers before preparing an indictment or planning the trial strategy.

Care should be taken, however, to avoid creating an unintended agency relationship between law enforcement and a private citizen employee who has or is considering handling potential digital evidence.

One advantage of inquiring about these issues is to ensure the proper collection of digital evidence when law enforcement becomes involved in a case. If the evidence is still on the original medium but the initial procedure used to gather the information was less than ideal, law enforcement may be in a position to resolve evidentiary issues even if they cannot perform their own collection process.

To reinforce adherence to traditional chain-of-custody procedures, law enforcement investigating a case should ask the following questions to determine how evidence was handled before they became involved.

1. What types of digital evidence have been collected prior to the involvement of law enforcement? For example, in a cyberstalking case, does a hardcopy (printed) version of the e-mail exist? Is an electronic copy available? Does it contain full header information?

2. Who handled the evidence?

   a. Document the name and job function of each individual who handled the digital evidence. Be aware that more than one person could be involved in this process.

   b. Identify everyone who had control of the digital evidence after it was examined and before it was given to law enforcement.

3. How was the digital evidence collected and stored?

   a. Identify all tools or methods used to collect the digital evidence.

   b. Determine who had access to the digital evidence after it was collected—anyone with access to the evidence should be considered part of the chain of custody. Account for all storage of data.

4. When was the evidence collected? Document the date and time when the evidence was gathered (including a reference to time zone if necessary). Careful ***documentation*** will enable the prosecutor and the prosecution witnesses to use a timeline to demonstrate the collection of evidence during its introduction and explanation at trial. Keep in mind that the collection of evidence might be an ongoing process.

5. Where was the evidence when it was collected?

In addition to the traditional "where" questions (e.g., "in which room was the computer found?"), other issues related to digital evidence can arise. Be aware that digital evidence may exist in more than one location simultaneously (e.g., e-mail may be located on the sender's computer, the recipients' computers, and their respective ISPs). Consider the following questions:

- What kind of machine/device held the digital evidence (is a serial number present)?

- Who had access to the machine/device?

- Who owned the machine/device?

- Was the machine/device shared?

- Was information retrieved from a network?

- Was information password protected?

- Who had access to password-protected information?

- Is the data located at an offsite location?

NOTE: For information about crime scene management, refer to the NIJ guide *Electronic Crime Scene Investigation: A Guide for First Responders* (www.ojp.usdoj.gov/nij/pubs-sum/187736.htm).

III. Building the record to make the case

A. Documentation

Thorough and accurate documentation of the evidence is critical. It is essential to establish both admissibility (under the principles discussed in chapters 1 and 3 of this guide) and the persuasive force of the evidence. A well-documented case is much more likely to result in a guilty plea, saving valuable prosecutorial and court resources. The previous chapter describes the information that law enforcement should gather to document what happened with respect to the data before seizure. Law enforcement also must thoroughly document its own actions with respect to the data. Documentation should include the steps taken to acquire, examine, and store the data.

With respect to examination notes, keep the following in mind:

- Comply with agency policy with regard to preparation and retention of notes.

- Be aware that retained notes and other records may be discoverable. The prosecutor must be notified and given an opportunity to review them.

- Do not commingle notes from different cases.

B. Reports and additional materials

1. Prepare a detailed report.

   Legal requirements for preparing and disclosing reports vary among jurisdictions and also are different for civil and criminal proceedings.

   a. See rule 26, Federal Rules of Civil Procedure.

   b. See rule 16, Federal Rules of Criminal Procedure.

   NOTE: Federal Rules of Civil Procedure can be viewed at www.law.cornell.edu/rules/frcp/overview.htm and Federal Rules of Criminal Procedure can be viewed at www.law.cornell.edu/rules/frcrmp.

2. Be prepared to provide the following if a witness is to be qualified as an expert or otherwise entitled to render an opinion:

   a. The basis for that opinion.

   b. The witness's curriculum vitae.

   c. A list of previous instances in which the witness has been qualified as an expert. The prosecutor should also be made aware of any instances in which the witness has been tendered as an expert but has not been qualified.

   NOTE: A witness who is not being offered as an expert might not be required under the law to produce a report. However, failure to adequately document pertinent information can affect the success of a prosecution.

IV. Returning original evidence

The person from whom electronic evidence has been seized may seek its return whether or not the examination has even been started. Some issues that may arise are outlined below.

A. Contraband

1. If the data seized are contraband, consider whether it is appropriate to return the media.

2. If the court, or local practice, determines that the original should not be provided to the defense, it may become necessary to provide the defense with access to the original or a forensic clone. Prepare in advance to be able to provide the defense with appropriately controlled access to seized evidence.

B. Stipulations

1. Seek stipulations as necessary regarding potentially disputed issues, such as authenticity, accuracy, ownership, hearsay, and chain of custody, when evidence is going to be returned. Remember that the stipulation needs to be obtained from the defense; a stipulation obtained from the owner of the data (e.g., a corporation) who is not the defendant is not binding on the defendant.

2. Anticipate that an ongoing business may need its information returned. If the information will be obtained with a search warrant, address this in the affidavit.

V. Obligations to disclose evidence to the defense

Discovery rules obligate the prosecution to provide evidence to the defense on a continuing basis. In addition, defense attorneys may seek to compel access to the evidence for a defense examiner to analyze.

A. General discovery

1. Provide *duplicate digital evidence* to the defense or accommodate its examination.

   a. The defense may be entitled to access to the actual evidence or to an image or a copy (depending on the circumstances). Be prepared to address (e.g., protective orders) defense demands for access to contraband.

   b. The defense may be entitled to examine the digital evidence on law enforcement premises.

      (1) Provide the defense with access to a clean computer to examine the digital media (no remnants from other cases should remain on that computer).

      (2) Provide the defense with an appropriate space to review the digital media.

2. Know the public document retention periods. (Be aware that State or Federal freedom of information statutes may be used as an alternative process to obtain information.)

3. Identify all the examiners who worked on and found the evidence.

B. Exculpatory material

The prosecution has an obligation to identify, preserve, and reveal exculpatory evidence to the defense. Those obligations vary according to jurisdiction, but typically require at a minimum that exculpatory evidence be made available to the defense in advance of trial and whenever discovered.

The prosecutor should determine whether the examiner looked for all relevant evidence, including that which could potentially be exculpatory. Failure to look for and report all relevant evidence may affect the credibility of the examiner's testimony, especially if additional information is found by a defense examination of the same media. Procedures should be in place to examine voluminous amounts of electronic evidence analogous to

the sampling that a forensic accountant might conduct on books and records to satisfactorily conclude an audit of those records.

NOTE: Evidence should be handled carefully to avoid destroying exculpatory material or inviting unnecessary, time-consuming, and expensive litigation over the possibility that exculpatory evidence was lost during the collection or analytical processes.

Chapter 3. Courtroom Preparation and Evidence Rules

Several issues should be kept in mind when preparing to present a case that involves digital evidence. The most obvious point is that the presentation of digital evidence requires familiarity with specialized, evolving, and sometimes complex technology. Therefore, it is essential that investigators and prosecutors:

- Acquire a basic working knowledge of the technical aspects of digital evidence in general.

- Master the specific technical details of the case at hand.

Because effective trial preparation begins at the outset of the investigation, the need for technical competence runs throughout the case. Issues pertinent to the search for, seizure of, and chain of custody of digital evidence are discussed in chapters 1 and 2 of this guide.

This chapter focuses on three aspects of pretrial preparation:

- Preliminary considerations that the prosecutor needs to take into account when reviewing the scope of the investigation to date.

- Effective pretrial communication among prosecutors, investigators, and examiners.

- Evidentiary issues (e.g., authentication and hearsay).

I. Preliminary considerations

Ideally, cases involving digital evidence should be developed by a team that consists of the prosecutor, lead investigator, and the examiner. Such cases often present special procedural and substantive issues.

One of the prosecutor's first tasks on being assigned the case is to review the scope of the investigation. Several key issues include:

A. Preparing and presenting an understandable theory of the case to the trier of fact.

B. Clarifying the nature of the technological issues.

1. Is the digital evidence associated with a ***"high-technology" crime***?

2. Although the case might not involve a high-technology crime, is digital evidence nevertheless an important aspect of the case? Or is digital evidence simply involved in the investigation or presentation of the case? (For example, a prosecutor may use a computer simulation or animation to illustrate an expert's testimony.)

C. Identifying and explaining the source and nature of the digital evidence in the case.

1. Do the storage devices contain evidence of the crime or are they themselves evidence or instrumentalities of the crime?

2. What hardware, software, operating systems, and system configurations were used by the target of the investigation or by the victim?

3. Was the evidence found on a stand-alone personal computer or a network?

D. Considering whether additional sources of digital evidence should be investigated (e.g., backup files, log files).

E. Considering all appropriate charges (e.g., does a child pornography possession case also involve dissemination charges?).

II. Pretrial communication

In addition to working as a team during the investigation stage of a digital evidence case, the prosecutor, investigator, and examiner should meet well in advance of trial to plan the presentation of the case. A prosecutor should consider the following key issues:

A. Discuss any points for which clarification, further analysis, or additional investigation may be needed.

1. Ensure familiarity with the specific technological aspects of the case.

2. Review the experience and qualifications of the investigator and examiner.

3. Review the scope and limitations of the evidence.

4. Read the reports prepared by the investigator and examiner before the meeting and use the meeting to clarify any points of uncertainty.

B. Conduct a pretrial meeting with the investigator and examiner to clarify the legal theory of the case, the elements of the crimes charged, and any anticipated defenses.

C. Review with the investigator and examiner the likely scope and direction of direct and cross-examination.

D. Distinguish the types of digital evidence.

Three broad categories of digital evidence raise issues that are especially important to address in a pretrial meeting—background evidence, substantive evidence, and illustrative evidence. Each category of evidence also requires clarifying whether a witness will testify as an expert.

1. Background evidence on technological issues.

   Provide background evidence when necessary to enable the trier of fact to understand the technical issues in the case. The following are examples of tactical questions to ask during the pretrial meeting:

   a. Will the examiner be asked to provide general background testimony as well as testimony concerning the results of his or her analysis?

   b. Are there general technical issues that are not in dispute? If so, can they be presented at the outset on a stipulated basis apart from the case-specific testimony?

   c. Does the use of metaphors or analogies to illustrate the technological issues present any legal complications? Using metaphors may have unintended consequences (e.g., referring to computers or computer files as "containers" may have Fourth Amendment implications).

   d. Should a stipulated glossary of undisputed technical terms be provided to the trier of fact?

2. Substantive evidence.

   The presentation of substantive evidence raises tactical and technical considerations.

   a. Tactical considerations.

      ■ Should e-mail messages and other digital evidence be presented in hard copy or on screen?

      ■ Will the jury be able to review hard copies of digital evidence in the jury room?

      ■ Should all relevant files or only specific examples be offered? If all are to be offered, should all of them or only specific examples be discussed? How should sample files (e.g., files in a child pornography case) be selected?

      ■ Digital evidence may include voluminous records for which summaries may be appropriate.

   NOTE: Live online activity at trial can be unpredictable. Consider capturing the activity outside of court using a screen capture program and playing that back in court. If a live demonstration is necessary, rehearse it carefully and anticipate what can go wrong.

   b. Technical considerations.

      ■ Addressing technical glitches during trial (e.g., arrange for technical support, provide backup or hard copies).

- ■ Preparing the courtroom for presentation of digital evidence.

  - Ensure the computers are functional.

  - Check that adequate and appropriate equipment is available and in working order, and that wiring and functional outlets are in place.

  - Notify court security that special equipment will be in the courtroom.

  - Notify the court reporter if audio will be presented.

  - Consider the placement of monitors and lighting issues.

- ■ Presenting the evidence.

  - Have clean copies of exhibits.

  - Ensure adequate setup time.

  - Ensure that standby mode, startup screen, sound (if applicable), and screen savers are deactivated.

  - Remember where presentation ended at the last break (i.e., cueing).

  - Create an adequate court record by fully describing referenced exhibits. Consider asking the court to allow nontraditional means of recording the presentation of evidence (e.g., videotape of computer presentations, printouts of screen captures, CD-ROMs).

  - Provide jury notebooks or exhibit books.

  - Consider whether to request jury note taking.

3. Illustrative evidence.

   In addition to the foregoing sets of tactical and technical issues, illustrative evidence may present additional considerations, such as:

   a. Which presentation medium or combination of media will be most persuasive.

   b. Whether to present animation in a fixed form that cannot be altered to accommodate changed assumptions or in a form that can be modified.

   c. Whether such evidence will need to be disclosed pretrial.

E. Consider pretrial rulings

Because digital evidence may be unfamiliar to the court and may seem complex, consider resolving admissibility (e.g., of expert testimony) and presentation issues by pretrial motion. This serves the following goals:

1. Avoids addressing those issues for the first time at trial before the jury.

2. Educates the court about technology-related issues.

3. Secures admission of evidence at trial.

4. Identifies potentially objectionable evidence.

III. Evidentiary considerations

Although the rules of evidence in State courts vary from jurisdiction to jurisdiction, many States' rules are modeled after the **Federal Rules of Evidence (FRE)**. Because a State-by-State review is beyond the scope of this guide, this section is based primarily on the FRE. Prosecutors should also consult whatever local rules apply.

> NOTE: The Federal Rules of Evidence can be viewed at www.law.cornell.edu/rules/fre/overview.html. A comprehensive analysis of Federal evidentiary rules can be found in *Searching and Seizing Computers and Obtaining Electronic Evidence in Criminal Investigations* (www.cybercrime.gov/s&smanual2002.htm).

Like other kinds of evidence, digital evidence can present issues such as relevance, authentication, and hearsay. Although these issues are usually resolved on the same basis as for other kinds of evidence, some points specific to digital evidence should be kept in mind. In addition to the digital evidence itself, the presentation of such evidence may involve expert testimony and its associated evidentiary issues. Although admissibility is ultimately a legal matter for the prosecutor to address, it may be helpful for the investigator and examiner to have a basic grasp of what will be required to establish admissibility.

Evidentiary considerations may be affected by the nature and source of the digital evidence. This section discusses the following:

- Defining evidentiary terms.

- Preexisting substantive evidence stored on a computer.

- Preexisting substantive evidence generated by a computer.

- Substantive and illustrative computer-generated evidence prepared for trial.

- Expert testimony.

A. Defining evidentiary terms

1. Judicial discretion (broad).

   Trial judges exercise broad discretion when ruling on admissibility of evidence. Because digital evidence may be unfamiliar terrain for many trial judges, proponents should be knowledgeable about how the rules of evidence apply to new technologies.

2. Relevance (does the evidence help?).

If the evidence helps to prove or disprove some fact that matters in the case, it normally will be admitted. The general approach of the FRE is that "[a]ll relevant evidence is admissible," unless some specific rule, statute, or constitutional provision excludes it (FRE 401). "Relevant evidence" is broadly defined to mean "evidence having any tendency to make the existence of any fact that is of consequence to the determination of the action more or less probable than it would be without the evidence" (FRE 401).

Of the various relevance-based objections, two are of particular concern:

a. Prejudice.

Relevant evidence may be excluded if the judge determines it is unduly prejudicial; that is, if its "probative value is substantially outweighed by the danger of unfair prejudice, confusion of the issues, or misleading the jury, or by considerations of undue delay, waste of time, or needless presentation of cumulative evidence" (FRE 403). These potential objections should be kept in mind when considering offering computer-generated simulations or animations into evidence.

b. Other actions.

Objections to evidence of "other crimes, wrongs, or acts" under FRE 404(b) can arise in digital evidence cases. However, such evidence may be admissible to prove "motive, opportunity, intent, preparation, plan, knowledge, identity, or absence of mistake or accident."

For example, a child pornography case may involve multiple wrongful acts, only some of which have been charged. Evidence of uncharged acts may be admissible to prove knowledge or absence of mistake.

3. Authentication (is it what you say it is?).

The evidence offered must be shown to be what its proponent claims it is (FRE 901(a)). The proponent is not required to rule out all possibilities that are inconsistent with authenticity. The standard for admission is a reasonable likelihood that the evidence is what it purports to be.

4. Hearsay (the preference for live testimony).

The rule against hearsay reflects a preference for having human statements intro-duced through live testimony in court, where the demeanor of the person making a statement (called the "declarant") can be observed by the trier of fact and he or she can be subjected to cross-examination. Digital evidence sometimes raises hearsay issues. A simplified but useful framework for considering hearsay problems follows:

a. Is it hearsay?

(1) Does the item fit within the core definition of hearsay?

"Hearsay" is an out-of-court statement that is offered to prove the truth of the matter asserted in the statement (FRE 801(c)). If the statement is not offered to

prove the truth of what it says, then it is not hearsay. For example, in a prosecution for credit fraud, computer printouts related to the defendant's accounts, kept by the collections department of the credit card company, would meet the core definition of hearsay because they would be offered to prove the truth of their contents. On the other hand, in a prosecution for online solicitation of a minor, the reply e-mails from the victim, if introduced simply to show contact between the defendant and victim rather than for the truth of their contents, would not meet the core definition of hearsay. They would be relevant for the fact that the defendant received them, not for what they say.

Another issue, apart from whether the evidence is offered to prove the truth of the matter asserted, is whether it constitutes a "statement" for hearsay purposes. A "statement" is defined as "(1) an oral or written assertion, or (2) nonverbal conduct of a person, if it is intended by that person as an assertion" (FRE 801(a)). The critical question in that regard, as discussed below, is often whether the record is computer generated (likely not a statement) or computer stored (may include statements).

(2) Even if the item falls within the core definition of hearsay, is it nevertheless *exempted* from the definition under the rules of evidence?

The FRE specify several categories of statements that, although offered to prove the truth of the matter asserted, are nevertheless deemed not to be hearsay. A common exemption for present purposes is the category of "admissions" (FRE 801(d)(2)).

b. If it is hearsay, is it nevertheless admissible under one of the exceptions?

Even if the statement qualifies as hearsay, it may nevertheless be admissible under one of the numerous exceptions to the hearsay rule. A common exception concerning digital evidence is the business records exception discussed below in section III.B.3.

B. Preexisting substantive evidence stored on a computer

1. Distinguishing substantive from illustrative evidence and computer-stored from computer-generated evidence.

   a. Substantive versus illustrative.

   As is the case with evidence in other forms, such as documents or live testimony, the principles applicable to the admissibility of digital evidence will depend in large part on where it comes from, how it was created, and the purpose for which it is offered. For present purposes, the term "substantive evidence" refers to evidence introduced for what it helps to prove itself, as opposed to "illustrative evidence," which refers to evidence that illustrates testimony but does not by itself prove anything.

   For example, computerized bank records in a credit card fraud case, e-mails in a cyberstalking case, and image files in a child pornography case are all substantive evidence. Each has substantive value in helping to prove an issue in the case. By

contrast, a computer animation used to illustrate a witness's testimony is offered to support the related substantive evidence (the testimony) rather than as proof of something itself.

b. Computer-stored versus computer-generated.

Computer-stored evidence includes documents and other records that were created by a human being and that just happen to be stored in electronic form. Examples include word-processing files and e-mail and Internet chat room messages. This kind of evidence may raise both authentication and hearsay issues.

Computer-generated evidence consists of the direct output of computer programs. Examples include the login record of an ISP, automated telephone call records, and automatic teller receipts. These records raise authentication issues but are not properly regarded as hearsay because they are not the statement of a person.

Finally, some records may contain a combination of computer-stored and computer-generated evidence. For example, a financial spreadsheet contains both the input data that originated from a person and the output of the computer program. Thus, such evidence presents both kinds of issues.

Another category of evidence, computer-generated evidence prepared for trial, also presents distinct issues that are discussed in section III.D below.

2. Authentication of computer-stored substantive evidence.

As stated previously, the authentication requirement simply means that the prosecution must show that the records stored in a computer are what the prosecution claims. Key issues usually center on identifying the author or authors of the computer-stored record and showing that it has not undergone significant change in any respect that matters in the case. Both of these points can often be shown through the chain of custody and other circumstantial evidence (some of which are discussed in chapter 2). Illustration (b)(1) of FRE 901 provides for authentication through "testimony of [a] witness with knowledge" that "a matter is what it is claimed to be."

Many courts have recognized that, while the witness called to establish authenticity must have personal knowledge of the facts about which he or she testifies, the witness need not have been the programmer of the computer in question, have knowledge of its maintenance and technical operation, or have seen the data entered. For example, computer-stored records of illegal drug transactions, found on a computer seized from a defendant's possession, could be authenticated by testimony from both the investigating officer who seized the computer (showing that the computer was indeed found in the defendant's possession and that names used in the files matched those associated through other evidence with the drug transactions) and the examiner who recovered the files (showing that the records are actually those found on the computer).

In some cases, because of the relative anonymity of some computer-stored records (such as those involving Internet-related crimes), establishing authorship may depend largely on circumstantial evidence. For example, in a child pornography case involving Internet chat rooms, evidence obtained from the defendant's residence that linked him

to his postings to the chat room, information he gave to an undercover officer, and information obtained from the ISP were sufficient to show authorship.

Authentication of digital evidence under the FRE is often a simple and straightforward matter. Defendants will sometimes challenge authenticity by alleging that the computer records could have been altered after they were created. Such arguments emphasize the ease with which computer records may be modified. Under the "reasonable likelihood" threshold for authentication, however, courts have generally not been receptive to such claims in the absence of specific evidence of alteration. Moreover, authentication of data may not necessarily be precluded by the use of examination software that alters nonessential data but does not effect significant changes to substantive data. For example, alteration of time and date stamps may not preclude admission in a given case.

Other issues that may be raised, apart from the possibility of tampering, include the completeness of the record, the input procedures, and the input method (accurate data conversion). If these matters are genuinely at issue, the prosecution should be prepared to present witnesses to address them.

Common ways to authenticate e-mail, for example, include:

- The chain of custody following the route of the message, coupled with testimony that the alleged sender had primary access to the computer on which the message originated.

- The content of the e-mail refers to matters of which the writer would have been aware.

- The recipient used the reply function to respond to the e-mail; the reply may include the sender's original message.

- After receiving the e-mail, the sender takes action consistent with its content.

In the majority of cases, a combination of circumstantial evidence provides the key to establishing the authorship and authenticity of a computer record.

3. Hearsay and computer-stored substantive evidence.

If the computer-stored record contains statements made by a person and is offered to prove the truth of the matter asserted in a statement, then the prosecution must consider the hearsay rule. As mentioned above, if the statement qualifies as an admission by a party-opponent, then FRE 801(d)(2) takes it out of the definition of hearsay and no exception is necessary. The hearsay rule also does not apply if the statement is not offered to prove the truth of the matter asserted.

The most common hearsay exception for computer-stored records is the business records exception (FRE 803(6)). To establish the foundation for this exception, the prosecution should be prepared to show that the source of information or the method or circumstances of preparation are trustworthy. This may be accomplished by showing that:

a. The computer equipment (hardware and software) on which the record was stored is recognized as standard in the field or reliable.

b. The data were entered in the regular course of business at or reasonably near the time of the occurrence of the event recorded.

c. The sources on which the record was based, as well as the method and time of preparation, indicate the record is trustworthy and its admission is justified.

This foundation may be established through the testimony of the custodian of the record or by a person who is familiar with the methods by which it was prepared, even if that person does not have personal knowledge of the underlying facts contained in the record and is not a computer expert familiar with the technical aspects of the software or hardware. In support of establishing trustworthiness, the prosecution might show:

- Company reliance on the data.

- Protection of the accuracy of data entry.

- Prevention of loss or alteration of the data while in storage.

- Provision for integrity of data output.

There is considerable overlap between the foundation required for authentication and the foundation required to establish the availability of the business records exception to the hearsay rule. As noted above in connection with authentication, allegations of some inaccuracies in the printouts of the computer records or in the records themselves will not necessarily defeat admissibility, provided an adequate foundation has been established. As is the case with paper business records, the presence of some inaccuracies goes to the weight rather than the admissibility of the records. Note also that, although records that are prepared solely for purposes of litigation may be challenged as untrustworthy, this limitation applies to the underlying data and not to the printout of records. Thus, preparation of a printout for purposes of litigation does not render it untrustworthy if the underlying data were entered and stored in the normal course of business.

For example, a defendant was prosecuted for concealing assets during a bankruptcy proceeding and destroying or concealing the bankrupt company's records. The trial court properly admitted computer printouts of the company's general ledgers, which contained inventory, payroll, and other accounting data entered by bookkeepers, after the prosecution called one of the bookkeepers to testify that the bookkeepers entered the data on a current basis, the printout accurately reflected the data, the printout was produced routinely each month, the data were regularly audited for accuracy, and the systems used were standard in the industry.

NOTE: Like any other record, computer-stored records can involve multiple levels of hearsay. The act of data entry is itself an out-of-court "statement" under FRE 801(a), but the result is usually the records kept in the regular course of business under FRE 803(6) as noted above. The underlying data entered may also contain hearsay "statements," which must qualify in turn for a hearsay exception or exemption.

4. Printouts of computer-stored substantive evidence.

    a. Requirement of the original, or best evidence, rule.

The so-called "best evidence" rule generally requires a party seeking to prove the contents of a writing, recording, or photograph to introduce the original writing, recording, or photograph unless an exception applies (FRE 1002).

Even though a printout of a computer-stored record might technically not be viewed as an original (especially because the "original" data are simply a string of 1s and 0s), the best evidence rule does not present a problem if the printout accurately reflects the data. In recognition of the demands of practicality and common usage, the FRE provide that "[i]f the data are stored in a computer or similar device, any printout or other output readable by sight, shown to reflect the data accurately, is an 'original'" (FRE 1001(3)). This principle applies even if the **duplicate** originals have an inconsistent appearance (e.g., different fonts or margins).

    b. Summaries.

Under FRE 1006, if the contents of voluminous writings, recordings, or photographs cannot be conveniently examined in court, a party may present them in the form of a chart, summary, or calculation—subject to limitations such as making the originals or duplicates available to the other party for inspection or copying. A printout of a computer record is not automatically regarded as a summary of that record.

Digital evidence, however, can be so voluminous that a summary of the data is required for convenience. For example, a summary of computerized invoices in a complex fraud case may be admissible if the limitations of FRE 1006 are met.

Some States have statutes that deal with the best evidence rule in more detail (e.g., California Evidence Code, sections 1521 through 1523).

C. Preexisting substantive evidence generated by a computer

Some computer records are generated by a computer program itself (rather than created by humans) and simply stored in electronic form. As used in this sense, the term "computer generated" refers to the record itself rather than the printout. (Note that many courts will loosely refer to the printout as computer generated regardless of whether the record that was printed resulted from human data entry or was created by a computer algorithm.) Examples of computer-generated records include automated telephone records, ISP logs, and automatic teller records.

Although some courts are beginning to recognize that not all digital evidence is alike, the proponent should be knowledgeable about the difference between computer-stored and computer-generated evidence. Correctly regarded, computer-generated evidence raises authentication issues but is not hearsay. Nevertheless, some courts continue to apply hearsay rules to computer-generated evidence. As a practical matter, this distinction may not make much difference at trial because of the overlap between authentication and establishment of the foundation for the business records exception.

1. Authentication of preexisting substantive evidence generated by a computer.

    Because computer-generated records are created directly by computer programs rather than by human input, authentication issues do not include identity of the records' author. Rather, the central authentication concerns are the reliability of the processing and output functions. Particularly pertinent to these concerns is FRE 901(b)(9), which provides for authentication by "[e]vidence describing a process or system used to produce a result and showing that the process or system produces an accurate result."

2. Hearsay and preexisting substantive evidence generated by a computer.

    A record that is generated by a computer program is not properly regarded as hearsay. This is because it does not meet the definition of a "statement" under FRE 801(a); it is neither "an oral or written assertion" nor "nonverbal conduct of a person if it is intended as an assertion." Further, FRE 801(b) defines a "declarant" as "a person who makes a statement." Some computer-generated records may have the appearance of a statement by a person, such as the "You've got mail" prompt that signals the presence of unopened e-mail, but these are actually only the automatic output of the computer program.

    The rationale for the hearsay rule—the preference for testing the trustworthiness of human assertions through in-court testimony subject to cross-examination and observation of witness demeanor by the trier of fact—does not apply to evidence generated directly by a nonhuman source. Thus, courts have long recognized that evidence such as the output of a Breathalyzer machine, a radar speed detection device, and a bloodhound's response to a scent raise authentication issues but are not hearsay.

    Some courts also have recognized that computer-generated records are not hearsay. Jurisdictions that fail to recognize this distinction have nevertheless tended to admit such evidence if an otherwise proper foundation has been laid under the business records exception. For example, a computer-generated record that an ATM safe had been opened was held admissible under the business records exception upon testimony by the records custodian, even though the custodian was unfamiliar with the functioning and accuracy of the program that generated the record as required for authentication purposes under FRE 901(b)(9).

D. Substantive and illustrative computer-generated evidence prepared for trial

1. Types of evidence.

    The two kinds of digital evidence discussed earlier—computer-stored records and computer-generated records—existed in some form before the investigation and prosecution commenced. That form may have been digital, so the evidence was reduced to hard copy for purposes of investigation and trial, but the underlying data existed beforehand. To that extent, substantive digital evidence is like other types of substantive evidence, such as fingerprints, biological samples, counterfeit currency, and murder weapons.

Other kinds of evidence are prepared for purposes of trial. Some of them are illustrative rather than substantive. A common example would be the diagram of a building used to illustrate a witness's testimony. Such a diagram proves nothing by itself; it is used only to illustrate the testimony.

Other types of evidence prepared for investigation and trial are substantive in that they prove something independently of a witness's testimony. An example would be photographs of a crime scene. Such evidence is "demonstrative" rather than "real." It is relevant for what it depicts but itself is not a thing involved in the transaction or occurrence that gives rise to the prosecution.

Similarly, computer-generated evidence that is prepared for trial can be either illustrative or substantive. A computer can be used to display any of the images that previously have been displayed by paper medium, such as a building floor plan (e.g., to show the positions of the perpetrator and witnesses in a robbery), an outline of the prosecution's case, or the highlights of an expert witness's testimony.

An example of a computer-generated static image used as substantive evidence is a digital picture of a crime scene or a perpetrator. Computers also allow manipulation of static images for emphasis and effect, such as zooming and highlighting, which previously had been done manually with paper images. Computer technology also allows the presentation of moving images.

For example, a forensic pathologist might use animation to illustrate the trajectory of a bullet through a murder victim's body. Just as videotape technology allowed litigants to create vivid depictions, such as "day-in-the-life" portrayals in personal injury cases, computer technology now permits sophisticated "re-creations" of events and computer simulations.

2. Evidentiary issues.

   a. Relevance.

     The primary relevance concern with computer-generated evidence for trial is FRE 403, which confers broad discretion on the trial judge to exclude evidence on the grounds of unfair prejudice, confusion of issues, or misleading the jury. For example, a computer-generated exhibit, especially an animated re-creation or simulation, might make such a powerful impression on the trier of fact as to risk undue prejudice. A trial judge who admits a computer-generated exhibit over an FRE 403 objection might give the jury a limiting instruction about the purpose for which the exhibit is admitted.

   b. Manner of interrogation.

     The normal manner of proceeding on direct examination is to ask the witness specific, nonleading questions. Counsel using computer-generated exhibits at trial should take care to coordinate them with proper questioning of witnesses and establish the proper foundation to avoid objections that the exhibit is essentially a lengthy narrative or in a sense leads the witness. These concerns are especially likely to arise if the evidence includes a voice-over narration.

c. Authentication and other foundation issues.

Images used to illustrate a witness's testimony are easy to authenticate, usually requiring only the witness's testimony that, based on personal knowledge, the image is a fair and accurate portrayal of what it represents. Digital photographs offered as pictures of a crime scene should normally be authenticated as conventional photographs would be, unless some real concern arises regarding alteration. For example, enhancing digital images may raise authentication issues. Re-creations and simulations that accompany expert testimony may require the same foundation as the expert testimony itself (see section III.E, below) to support the assumptions on which such evidence rests. Testimony that the input and output parameters were correct may also be needed. For example, simulations are commonly used in civil cases to portray airline disasters and automobile crashes. Authentication issues in such cases focus on the extent to which input data correspond to actual events (in terms of accuracy and completeness) and the scientific validity of the mathematical model underlying the simulation.

d. Hearsay.

(1) Is it hearsay?

Whether the computer-generated evidence prepared for trial raises hearsay issues depends on the purpose for which it is introduced and on the nature of the evidence. A computer exhibit used simply to illustrate a witness's testimony—such as the computer image of a building floor plan or a computer diagram of a handgun—is not offered to prove the truth of the matter asserted, or to prove anything. It is offered only to illustrate the witness's testimony. As such, it is not hearsay. A digital photograph of a crime scene, when offered as substantive proof, is not a "statement" but rather the direct output of a machine.

Re-creations or simulations, on the other hand, may go beyond the testimony of the witness and thus constitute substantive evidence apart from a live witness's testimony. Hearsay problems may arise if the simulation is based on out-of-court statements, including input data and assumptions that underlie the simulation.

(2) Is an exception available?

If a computer-generated exhibit is deemed hearsay, its proponent will either have to find an applicable exception or some other way around the hearsay rule.

Several exceptions might apply to the input data. Measurements, for example, might be regarded as "present sense impressions" under FRE 803(1); other data might be taken from business records that qualify under FRE 803(6) or public records that qualify under FRE 803(8). (Public records, however, are subject to important limitations in criminal proceedings.) Even if the input data qualify under one of those exceptions, however, the hearsay rule may still apply to the operation of the program and the output function.

The proponent of the exhibit might also try to invoke the so-called "residual exception" under FRE 807, which is subject to several limitations. The proponent must show that the "statement" is evidence of a material fact and is more probative of that fact than any other evidence the proponent could offer through reasonable efforts, and that admission of the evidence serves the purposes of the rules of evidence and the interests of justice. FRE 807 is also subject to a notice requirement.

The proponent of a computer animation or simulation prepared for trial might seek admission under FRE 703 (bases of opinion testimony by experts). Note, however, that the amendments enacted in 2000 to FRE 703 restrict the admissibility of otherwise inadmissible information relied on by the expert. Such evidence now is inadmissible unless the trial court finds that its "probative value in assisting the jury to evaluate the expert's opinion substantially outweighs [its] prejudicial effect."

E. Expert opinion testimony

Using opinions of an expert witness calls for a threefold approach:

- Identify the issues that will require an expert opinion (discussed in chapter 4, section III.A).

- Identify a qualified expert (discussed in chapter 4, section III.C).

- Ensure that the qualified expert will use an admissible method (discussed in this section).

Two primary tests (or some variant of them) govern the admission of the opinions of experts. One is the *Frye* test (*Frye* v. *United States*, 54 App. D.C. 46, 293 F. 1013 (1923)); the other is the *Daubert* test (*Daubert* v. *Merrell Dow Pharmaceuticals*, 509 U.S. 579 (1993)).

NOTE: The admissibility of expert opinion testimony may be challenged prior to trial. The prosecutor and the expert should prepare to meet the pretrial challenge as carefully as preparing for the trial itself.

---

1. *Daubert* governs in Federal Court.

Daubert has replaced the *Frye* test, both in Federal court and in many State courts, with a test where the trial judge determines the admissibility of expert opinion testimony based on its relevance and the reliability of the underlying scientific techniques. The U.S. Supreme Court suggested that whether scientific expert opinion evidence will be helpful to the trier of fact may turn on whether: (1) the scientific technique can be— and has been—tested; (2) the technique has been subjected to peer review and publication; (3) there is a known or potential rate of error; and (4) the technique has been generally accepted by the relevant scientific community.

The Court made clear in *Daubert* and subsequent cases that this list is neither a rigid nor an exhaustive set of requirements. *Daubert* is generally seen as the U.S. Supreme

Court's suggestion that trial courts act as "gatekeepers" to limit the admissibility of "junk science" and encourage the development of reliable scientific and technological forensic techniques. Recent changes to article seven of the FRE, which governs the admissibility of expert opinion testimony, are based on *Daubert* and its progeny. *Kumho Tire Co., Ltd.* v. *Carmichael* (526 U.S. 137 (1999)) extended *Daubert* to technical areas other than those considered strictly scientific.

Technical expert opinion testimony is admissible under FRE 702 (as amended in 2000) if "(1) the testimony is based upon sufficient facts or data, (2) the testimony is the product of reliable principles and methods, and (3) the witness had applied the principles and methods reliably to the case."

NOTE: The law concerning expert testimony continues to evolve. Numerous additional factors have been added by the lower courts to the four factors of *Daubert*. See *A Guide to Forensic Testimony: The Art and Practice of Providing Testimony as an Expert Technical Witness,* listed on page 61 of this guide.

---

2. Many States still use a version of the *Frye* test.

Frye allowed scientific techniques to be admitted in court if they are generally accepted within the relevant scientific community. As the Court of Appeals for the District of Columbia Circuit stated in *Frye*, "courts will go a long way in admitting expert testimony deduced from a well-recognized scientific principle or discovery, [but] the thing from which the deduction is made must be sufficiently established to have gained general acceptance in the particular field in which it belongs." (Note that under *Daubert*, general acceptance is only one of several factors for courts to consider.)

As examiners employ new software and updated versions of older software in their examination of digital media, they may face *Frye* or *Daubert* challenges to that software. As examination techniques develop and as expert witnesses deduce opinions about facts and evidence, "the thing from which the deduction is made must be sufficiently established" so as to be relevant and reliable in court.

NOTE: As discussed in chapter 4, sections I and II, even if a method that relied on technical or other specialized knowledge were used to locate or identify evidence, unless an expert is giving an opinion based on that method, the method does not have to meet the *Daubert* or *Frye* standard. Further, the mere fact that the evidence resulted from the output of a computer program (e.g., ATM records) does not mean the evidence must satisfy the requirements for scientific evidence.

Chapter 4. Presentation of Digital Evidence

A trial that involves digital evidence differs in two fundamental respects from most other trials. First, legal issues concerning the admissibility of digital evidence will nearly always arise. Those issues are discussed in chapter 3, "Courtroom Preparation and Evidence Rules." Second, a prosecutor's presentation of digital evidence may involve terms, issues, and concepts that are complex or unfamiliar. Therefore, the opening statement should be crafted to introduce the jury to the terminology and types of digital evidence that may be presented during the trial. Careful planning of case presentation and how digital evidence will be used throughout is essential to the successful outcome of a trial.

This chapter provides guidance on how to successfully present a case that involves digital evidence.

I. Educating the audience

If a case is complex, educate the audience—both the judge and the jury—at every stage of the litigation process:

- Pretrial hearings (including *Daubert* or *Frye* challenges).

- Jury selection.

- Opening statement.

- Witness testimony.

- Objections (both in making and answering them).

- Closing argument.

Although it is important to bring an audience up to a minimum level of competency or understanding, do not attempt to make them experts. The general rule of prosecution is to keep it simple. This holds especially true in the presentation of a case that is complex by nature.

II. What needs to be proved or disproved?

Every case requires a careful examination of the elements of the charges to ensure that convincing evidence will be presented on each element. Digital evidence cases often require a determination by the prosecutor of what can and should be eliminated as reasonable explanations for the evidence. The key questions to consider are:

- Can all reasonable alternative explanations be disproved?

- Is it necessary to disprove all alternative explanations?

A. Technical anomalies

In some instances, no complete or clearly adequate explanation can be found for a particular anomaly in the evidence. In other cases, the cost of explaining the anomaly (e.g., by a computer programmer or an electrical engineer) will be prohibitive as a practical matter.

As computers and operating systems have become more complex, most network administrators and computer maintenance personnel limit their problem solving to the most frequently recurring problems. Computer experts accept the existence of unexplained "bugs" or "glitches" without doubting the validity of information stored or processed by computers.

B. Disproving alternatives

What a prosecutor has to disprove depends on what issue is involved and the strength of the rest of the case.

When a crucial element is knowledge, such as in a case involving possession of child pornography, the prosecutor must be prepared to disprove defense claims that the pornography was stored on the defendant's computer without his knowledge. The prosecutor does not, however, need to disprove unreasonable alternatives (e.g., a power surge caused child pornography to appear on the computer).

C. "Timing is everything"

When to rebut a defense assertion is important. For example, if the defendant's knowledge of the contents of the computer will be crucial, it is sometimes wise to let the defendant raise the issue first and allow the evidence—through either cross-examination or rebuttal—to disprove the claim rather than assert the disproof in the case-in-chief. A jury often will attach more importance to issues raised in the State's case and hold the prosecutor to a higher standard than they will if the defense attorney has raised the issue and the prosecutor is merely attacking the defense argument.

III. Expert witnesses and technical evidence

A. Deciding whether a technical expert witness is needed

A major decision in cases that involve complex technology and extensive examination of digital evidence is whether to use an expert witness; that is, one qualified by special training, knowledge, or experience.

If the witness renders an opinion, he or she must be qualified as an expert. In some instances, a witness may testify to complex matters without having to qualify as an expert because the witness does not offer an opinion. Judges also may have differing

standards with regard to whether witnesses who offer nonopinion, technical testimony will be required to be qualified as an expert.

In many cases that involve digital evidence, either the investigator at the scene or an examiner can testify as to how the digital evidence was found. Although the examiner may have used expert skills and techniques, the only relevant issue at trial is whether the evidence in question was on the suspect's computer, not how it was found. Either it was or was not on the computer. Thus, for that question, the examiner is a fact witness.

Unless an expert is giving an opinion based on a method that relies on technical or other specialized knowledge, even if such knowledge was used to find or identify evidence, the method does not have to meet the *Daubert* or *Frye* standard discussed in chapter 3. For example, a metal detector may have been used to find spent cartridges at a crime scene, but the technology of metal detectors would not need to be qualified. Once the cartridges are found, the issue focuses on them. Cases that involve digital evidence may be similar.

B. Using technical fact witnesses and expert opinion witnesses effectively

Although an expert is not needed to explain how the cartridges or bullets were found in the metal detector example above, the opinion of an expert qualified in firearms and toolmark examination will be required to demonstrate whether the lands and grooves on a particular bullet can be matched to a bullet fired from the suspect weapon. Similarly, digital evidence cases may sometimes need expert opinion testimony.

C. Identifying a community of qualified technical experts

Although experts in digital evidence examination may lack the traditional trappings of other recognized disciplines, they may nevertheless be well qualified. In fact, practice-based qualifications can be superior to qualifications based only on graduate degrees and memberships in recognized professional peer groups. Whatever the credentials of the expert, be prepared to demonstrate knowledge and understanding of the matters about which the expert is testifying. When selecting prosecution experts to assist in investigations and to testify at trial, determine whether a recognized community of experts in the relevant area of expertise exists and how the candidate is evaluated within that community.

D. Explaining the issues in the case and the legal constraints for examining the available evidence

The prosecutor should ensure that the expert understands how the rules of evidence and procedure affect the admissibility, discoverability, and usefulness of the expert's observations and conclusions.

The expert may help the prosecution critique the evidence and determine whether a plea bargain is more appropriate than taking a particular case to trial.

E. Planning to deal with a *Daubert* gatekeeping challenge

The prosecutor should prepare the witness for meeting a *Daubert* or *Frye* challenge (see chapter 3 for details). Although this type of challenge is usually encountered in pretrial motions, it can also occur during the trial, either as an admissibility or credibility issue.

F. Preparing the witness for trial

Preparing a witness to testify about digital evidence involves all the considerations that apply in other cases as well as some special concerns. The following is a nonexclusive list of points to keep in mind:

1. Preparing for direct examination.

   a. The expert should assist the factfinder by adopting and maintaining an objective role at all times during the litigation process.

   b. The prosecutor should provide the witness with a copy of all relevant materials (e.g., police reports, forensic records, transcripts, defense materials, if any).

   c. The prosecutor should prepare the witness to testify at pretrial hearings (e.g., a *Daubert* hearing) about his or her qualifications and testimony and remind the witness that he or she will be asked again to testify before the jury about qualifications, opinion (if any), and the reason for that opinion.

   d. The prosecutor should suggest that the witness inform the prosecutor if he or she is contacted by the defense team.

   e. The prosecutor should encourage the witness to prepare his or her testimony on direct examination so that it is simple, understandable, and interesting. It may be helpful to use a "storytelling" approach.

   f. The prosecutor should inform the witness about the questions he or she will be asked on direct examination. The witness should tell the prosecutor about the exhibits he or she will be using, audiovisual equipment needs, and texts or articles on which he or she relied in preparing to testify.

   g. The witness should know that any materials he or she used to prepare testimony or will use during testimony may be subject to production to the defense.

   h. The witness should explain all technical terms and acronyms in simple language. For example: "I ran an MD5 hash algorithm against the forensic image and the hash values had not changed. This means that every file on the copy was identical to the file on the original."

   i. The witness should direct his or her testimony to the jury, not to the attorney asking the questions.

   j. The prosecutor should explain to the witness that the judge may limit the scope and nature of the testimony. The witness will have to testify within the limits established by the trial court.

k. An investigator who is identified as part of the prosecution team must nevertheless testify in an objective manner. To avoid appearing biased, the witness should be aware of his or her overall demeanor, including body language, tone of voice, and facial expressions, while testifying.

2. Preparing for cross-examination.

   a. The witness should never be combative on cross-examination. It alienates the jury and weakens his or her effectiveness.

   b. The witness should keep in mind: "Your testimony is not about you, it is about the evidence."

   c. The defense attorney will take control of cross-examination by asking leading questions; that is, questions that suggest their own answers. Do not avoid (or appear to avoid) answering the question. The witness should answer the *asked* question, not the *implied* question. For example:

   Attorney: "Isn't it true that you waited until 3 days after receiving the computer to book it into a secure evidence room?"

   Witness: "Yes."

   OR

   Witness: "Yes, and I can explain my answer if you'd like."

   BUT NOT:

   Witness: "I was scheduled to go on vacation, and the department refused to authorize the overtime, and . . . ."

   d. The witness should never compete with the defense attorney. The witness's demeanor on the stand on cross-examination should be the same as on direct examination. If the witness feels as though he or she is on trial rather than the defendant, this could indicate that the witness is trying to compete with the defense attorney. The witness should be reminded before trial that the prosecutor will have an opportunity to ask more questions on redirect examination. If the prosecutor and the witness have worked together as a team, the prosecutor should know how best to proceed following cross-examination.

3. Preparing for rebuttal.

Sometimes the defense calls its own witness or witnesses to address digital evidence offered by the government. These witnesses may be highly qualified professionals. In some cases, they may be professionals with legitimate forensic practices who may not have had access to all the relevant data. It is also possible that they are "professional" defense witnesses with no actual experience with forensic practices. After the defense witness testifies, the prosecution witness may be called back to rebut the testimony. This should be anticipated and prepared for prior to trial.

IV. Recurring issues in computer crime trials

Although each digital evidence case is different, some common issues arise with regard to both the basic elements of the crimes charged and the nature of computers and computer networks. These include the following:

A. Identity

Although the digital evidence may show that a crime was committed from the defendant's computer, the prosecution may need to directly connect the defendant to that computer. The defendant can be tied personally to information found on the computer in several ways, including the following:

1. Through confession or admission.

2. Circumstantially (e.g., the defendant was the only resident at the computer location, the defendant is the registered user of the hardware or software).

3. Through substantive information on the computer uniquely within the defendant's knowledge.

4. Through content analysis; i.e., establishing the existence of unique similarities between the grammar, spelling, or other characteristics of the evidence and other writing known to have been authored by the defendant.

B. Knowledge

In some cases, it may be necessary to show the defendant's knowledge of the digital evidence on the computer. For example, one common defense in cases involving possession of child pornography is the claim that the defendant was not aware the images were on his computer. Such a claim can often be disproved by:

1. The number of such images found.

2. The directory structure. Were the pictures placed in directories that were logically related to the pictures (e.g., C:\Pictures\young\girls\sex)?

3. File names. Are the file names unique, and do they accurately describe the contents of the files (e.g., 8yrold.jpg; baby.jpg)?

4. Other indications on the computer of the defendant's interest in child pornography, such as newsgroup subscriptions and history of Internet activity.

C. Chronology of events

Time and date stamps on files can be powerful evidence tying the defendant to the computer and the computer to the crime. Nevertheless, time and date stamps have limitations:

■ Their accuracy is directly dependent on the accuracy of the computer's internal clock.

- They are tied to a particular time zone.

- They can be easily manipulated.

The accuracy or inaccuracy of a time and date stamp can be shown in numerous ways, including the following:

1. **Consistent offsets.** Are the files consistently off by a specific amount of time or date (e.g., always 1 hour or 2 days off)? If that is the case, a persuasive argument can be made that the file times and dates can be adjusted by that offset and reflect accurate times and dates.

2. **Internal file accuracy.** Is the time and date on a file consistent with the contents of that file? For example, is the date stamp on a file of a letter consistent with the date in the introductory portions of that letter?

3. **Compare e-mail header dates with time and date stamps assigned by the system.** On e-mail systems in which e-mail is saved as individual files or has been copied to a file, is the time and date information in the header of the e-mail consistent with the time and date stamp the system assigned the file?

4. **Compare known times and dates with system-assigned times and dates.** Were files downloaded from the victim's computer at a known date and time? Do the files appear on the suspect's computer with time and date stamps consistent with that date and time?

5. **Networked computer.** Many networks are configured to automatically update a client's internal clock when the client is logged on. Is the computer in question a client on a network? Are the clocks on client computers on that network automatically updated?

6. **Patterns of file creation times and dates.** Is there a cluster of files created at the same time and date? The relative time and date (i.e., all created at the same time) may be more important than the absolute time and date of creation.

7. **Experiment.** Use the suspect's hardware, but not the original drive, to create and alter files. Observe the discrepancies, if any, and compare them with the evidence files.

NOTE: For further information about investigating computer crimes, see the other guides in this series:

- *Electronic Crime Scene Investigation: A Guide for First Responders* (www.ojp.usdoj.gov/nij/pubs-sum/187736.htm).

- *Forensic Examination of Digital Evidence: A Guide for Law Enforcement* (www.ojp.usdoj.gov/nij/pubs-sum/199408.htm).

- *Investigations Involving the Internet and Computer Networks* (www.ojp.usdoj.gov/nij/pubs-sum/210798.htm).

V. Jury selection

The prosecutor should consider carefully the kind of jurors who would be best for a computer crime case that involves the admission of complex or highly technical evidence. Investigators can assist prosecutors in developing appropriate questions and considering the makeup of the overall panel and the individual jurors who are called.

The goal is not to select technical experts to be jurors but to find at least a few people who have sufficient experience using computers to be able to follow the technical testimony that must be presented in the course of the trial. Ideally, one or more of these jurors will be able to assist the other jurors in understanding the evidence during deliberations after the case has been presented.

A. Jury selection

Depending on the case, crucial information from potential jurors in voir dire may be gleaned from answers to the following questions:

1. Do they have any type of visual impairment that would interfere with their ability to review materials on the computer monitor or on the projection screen?

2. What is their knowledge and experience level with computers?

3. Do they view digital evidence with suspicion?

4. Do they have strong views (either way) about the specific crime that is to be prosecuted?

5. Do they view victims of computer crimes, particularly business victims, as partially to blame?

6. What is their knowledge and level of experience with the Internet, e-mail, and other specific aspects of computers relevant to the case?

7. Has any of them ever been the victim of a crime similar to the one being prosecuted?

8. What security measures, if any, do they use for their own computer?

9. In intrusion cases, what are their views on privacy and assumption of the risk in using networked computers?

B. Special considerations for computer experts in the jury pool

It is not necessary that a computer expert be selected to be a juror. The presence of a computer expert on a jury is similar to the presence of a physician on a jury in a case in which medical testimony is relevant. Just as a physician may be able to explain complicated medical concepts, a computer expert may be able to clarify information technology issues to fellow jurors. However, just as a physician on the jury might require the government to overprove the prosecution's case and to disprove wholly immaterial matters, so might a computer expert substitute his or her knowledge for the evidence presented and dominate the deliberations concerning the forensic examinations and analyses.

VI. Presenting complicated and technical issues

The following are some useful methods for presenting complicated evidence in digital evidence or other complex cases.

A. Define technical words in terms and concepts the jury can understand.

Use simple analogies to explain general concepts (e.g., sending e-mail is like sending a postcard; it goes from the mailbox to the local post office through other post offices to the recipient's local post office and then to the recipient's mailbox), but keep in mind that because the digital world is so different from the real world, analogies may not be helpful. To make the analogy work, the real-world situation may have to be distorted to such an extent that it becomes unrealistic. As a result, the familiar situation to which one wishes to analogize becomes unfamiliar.

Furthermore, using analogies may have unanticipated legal consequences. For example, an analogy based on case law may import legal constraints that would be inappropriate for digital evidence.

Consider, for example, the analogy comparing peer-to-peer file sharing with a traditional library:

- There is an unlimited supply of each book.

- No book needs to be returned.

- The library patrons can place their own books in the library.

- The library patrons can take the books that they have checked out and put them in their own libraries, which then become available to other patrons.

In an effort to draw an accurate analogy between familiar libraries and peer-to-peer file sharing, a strange—and unfamiliar—library has been created. The addition of the necessary qualifications so reduces the points of correspondence of the purported analogy that the thing ultimately is said to be more like itself than anything else.

B. Use pictures, drawings, and/or graphs to demonstrate complex systems or concepts.

C. Build the knowledge of the jury through the opening statement and each successive layer of witnesses' testimony.

1. Introduce jurors to simple concepts, explain those concepts in detail, and then move to more complex issues that rely on understanding the initial concepts.

2. When possible, relate the technology in the case to the technology the jurors indicated in voir dire that they were familiar with or have used.

D. Review technological concerns regarding presentations.

The decision about what presentation technology to use is dictated by many factors, the most important of which is mastery of the presentation technology and time to adequately prepare and test the presentation. Keep in mind, however, that jurors, particularly younger ones and those who are familiar with technology-based presentations, may expect a visual or multimedia presentation.

If presentation technology will be used, keep the following in mind:

1. Communicate with the witness and the jury, not the computer. While this is true for most stages of a trial, it is most important during opening and closing arguments when you are talking directly to the jury.

    a. Have someone else control the computer if possible.

    b. Look at the jury, not at the screen.

2. Depending on the purpose of a slide, darken the screen when you are not directly using the information on it.

    a. During the trial, consider leaving an exhibit on the screen for an extended period of time if:

       (1) It is important for the jury or witness to be able to refer to the exhibit over time.

       (2) The continued display of the exhibit will have an (nonobjectionable) emotional impact.

    b. During a closing argument or at other times when the jury should remain focused on what the prosecutor or witness is saying, make the screen black.

3. Use presentation software for specific purposes (not simply because it is available), such as the following:

    a. To show graphics, animation, or effects uniquely suited to such software (but ensure the substance is relevant).

    b. To show or preserve organization in a complex presentation.

    c. For dramatic effect.

    d. To use the power of visuals.

    e. To focus the jury's attention.

    f. To show evidence word by word when effective (e.g., for the jury to read the text of an e-mail).

4. Do not use presentation software for the wrong reason or in the wrong way.

    a. Do not simply read what is on the screen.

b. Do not use it as a bullet outline for the closing argument.

c. Do not display text-heavy slides unless:

(1) The jury needs to read the text.

(2) The focus needs to be placed on the text.

d. Do not conceal part of a slide or show it quickly without giving the jury a chance to read it. Jurors in mock digital evidence trials uniformly have expressed the belief that attorneys who highlight only a portion of a document (thus obscuring the rest of it) or who flash documents on and off the screen quickly are doing so to hide something.

5. Follow basic presentation rules (always subject to exception):

a. Maintain consistency in appearance and layout.

b. Provide no less than 10 seconds and no more than 100 seconds per slide (use a black screen if there is a need to talk in between slides).

c. Use colors that work when projected (do not rely on how they look on a computer monitor). Some studies have shown that light blue text on a dark blue background is easiest to read, particularly in less-than-ideal lighting conditions.

d. Use sufficiently large fonts.

e. Do not use busy, rainbow, or ransom note slides.

VII. Closing argument

A. General reminders

Key points to remember when preparing a closing argument are summarized below.

1. Condense the theme of the case.

a. The theme of the case, which should have been articulated in the opening statement, should reverberate throughout the closing argument.

b. Have an opening and a closing to the closing argument—the first and last words said are the most remembered.

c. Know in advance what the jury should remember.

2. Include jury instructions.

a. Connect the argument to jury instructions at key points.

b. Remind the jury that the instructions also show what does not have to be proven.

3. Determine the "thrust" of the closing argument.

   a. One of the primary purposes of a closing argument is to make simple and clear that which seems complex.

   b. How emotional should the closing be?

   c. Emphasize strengths.

   d. Pounce on defense weaknesses.

4. Determine how to address defense arguments by answering the following questions.

   a. On what points should a defense argument be answered, and on what points should the jury be provided with ammunition to use in deliberations?

   b. Should all defense arguments be addressed, or should emphasis be placed only on the most relevant ones?

   c. How should defense arguments that are considered irrelevant be handled? Should they be ignored, should the jury be told that they are irrelevant, or should they be dismissed with an explanation as to their irrelevance?

   d. Should attention be drawn to irrelevant arguments by even mentioning them?

   e. Should defense arguments be diluted by mentioning, even briefly, irrelevant ones?

5. Determine the rebuttal.

   a. Should the agenda be followed? Respond point by point to defense arguments.

   b. Will sufficient time be allowed to prepare a theme-based rebuttal that adequately responds to defense arguments?

   c. If an agenda is followed, obviously do not ignore the defense arguments.

   d. Even if responding point by point, have prepared portions, explicitly including the final words of the argument, which return to the theme of the government's case.

B. Key points to remember when making a closing argument in a digital evidence case are:

1. Put the digital evidence in perspective by showing how nondigital evidence corroborates it and vice versa.

2. Review the more complex issues and evidence of the case.

   a. Remind the jury that they do not need to master the technology to understand the evidence.

   b. If "education witnesses" have been used correctly, the prosecutor will not need to explain or rehash.

3. Make connections that may not have been obvious and explain the significance of key evidence in light of the jury's newly acquired technological knowledge.

4. If a juror(s) has significant computer knowledge or experience, make a connection with that juror(s) during the portion of the closing argument where the significance of the evidence is explained.

   a. Evaluate whether the juror(s) appears to agree with the explanations.

   b. If the juror(s) appears to agree with the explanations, consider reminding the other jurors that if they did not completely understand some of the technological explanations, they can ask their fellow juror(s) to explain them.

Chapter 5. Application: Child Pornography

Child pornography and individuals who possess pictures or videos (collectively "images") that are sexually exploitative of children represent one of the darkest sides of the Internet. Investigating and prosecuting child pornography cases inevitably involves more than just the evidence that certain images were found on a computer used by the defendant.

Many such people are collectors of child pornography, and their computers and digital storage media are usually found to contain hundreds or even thousands of images. Information about the origin of some of the images or the identities of the children depicted may be determined during the investigation. Other images show the tragically countless and nameless child victims around the world whose pictures continue to pass from one perpetrator to the next.

Beyond having child pornography on their computers, some of these people also attempt to commit or may actually commit acts of physical sexual assault or abuse of children. A discussion of evidence in cases that involve physical acts against a child is outside the scope of this guide.

Child pornography investigations often involve people who are quite knowledgeable about technology, computers, and the Internet. They trade images with other collectors within their own towns and around the world using, for example, Web sites, file sharing, e-mail, buddy lists, password-protected files, or **encryption**.

Having a basic understanding of this subculture of the Internet and the persons who are its members will, in turn, help an investigator and prosecutor better understand the context within which to view and prosecute a particular case. Law enforcement investigators with experience or specialized training in pornography cases, as well as other investigative resources such as the National Center for Missing and Exploited Children, also may provide great assistance to a prosecutor.

I. Considerations: Investigative and forensic evidence

Child pornography investigations often start with a report to law enforcement by an independent third party who discovers what he or she believes to be child pornography on a computer or storage media while using or servicing computer equipment. Other child pornography cases may be byproducts of an undercover online investigation directed at child predators. The suspect may have sent child images to the undercover officer. Investigating officers at some point may have seized the suspect's computer and media, and the subsequent forensic examination may have disclosed child images. Whatever the background, a followup investigation that provides a good understanding

of the circumstances of the use of the computer and background details about the defendant will provide effective evidence for trial.

From the prosecution's perspective, these cases are often not just about the found images. A comprehensive forensic examination and analysis that reveal usage habits by the defendant or others who had access to the computer will help establish possession of the images and knowledge of what they depict. Because of this, the forensic examiner may prove a critical witness at trial.

The forensic examination may provide evidence in support of the prosecution of the case including, but not limited to:

- Internet browser history and typed **URLs**.

- Subscription-based Web sites.

- E-mail correspondence.

- File sharing or peer-to-peer software, usage history, and remnants.

- Instant messages.

- Buddy lists.

- Time/date stamps associated with files.

- Folder and directory structures (i.e., "path" to images and data).

- Screen names, e-mail addresses, online identities.

- Evidence of remote or offsite file storage locations (physical or virtual).

- Logon-logoff details.

- Internet service provider (ISP) information.

- Financial or other personal information related to interest in children.

- *Metadata* associated with the charged images.

The followup investigation may provide evidence for use at trial, including but not limited to:

- Whether images are from a series known to be of identifiable children (e.g., from databases maintained by the National Center for Missing and Exploited Children or U.S. Immigration and Customs Enforcement).

- Live witness testimony concerning actual identification of children shown in images.

- Whether defendant has a history of Internet postings (e.g., Web site, newsgroup, or bulletin board services) under various screen names or identities.

- Identification via ISP account information of the e-mail account or address association.

II. Considerations: charging

The upfront charging decisions made by a prosecutor in child image cases will likely have a significant impact on the subsequent trial. A practical approach to the charging decision might include basing counts on the images that give rise to the fewest legitimate legal or evidentiary challenges (e.g., video or still images, known victim series, basis for estimating age of unknown children, nature of conduct shown, showing of faces and other portions of body, background in image) and that also will have the greatest impact on the jury.

Thus, as the prosecutor in a child pornography case decides which of the many images should be used as the basis for the charges, the decision will involve both substantive and tactical considerations.

A. Substantive considerations

- Do the images meet the statutory definitions of child pornography or of obscenity?

- Which and how many of the recovered images will be used as the basis for the charges?

- Is the evidence adequately linked to the defendant (e.g., were the images recovered from a computer in the defendant's home or place of employment or were they found on external media (such as a CD-ROM or flash memory drive) and where was that media found?

- How are counts structured?

  - By image.

  - By event (e.g., download dates).

  - By storage media (e.g., diskette, hard drive, thumb drive, CD, DVD).

- How many counts will be charged? Does local law allow for the filing of individual counts or is there a multiplicity or duplication issue?

- Does the evidence establish that the images depict real children?

- Is the theory of the case based on possession alone or is there also evidence of distribution or promotion?

- Should the case be charged as an attempt instead of as a completed crime?

B. Tactical considerations

- How should the case be charged for best jury impact without overcharging?

- Can uncharged images and other related data be admitted as evidence of identification, intent, knowledge, ownership, control, or absence of mistake or negligence?

  - Is there evidence that the defendant is connected to a larger group of similarly interested persons with whom the defendant is in contact via computer?

– Is there evidence that suggests that the defendant is more than a collector (e.g., evidence of unknown child victims of actual physical sexual assault or abuse by the defendant)?

– Was other evidence recovered that demonstrates relevant proclivities of the defendant (e.g., sexually oriented magazines or video tapes, Internet search engine history, suggestive articles of clothing)?

– What evidence exists concerning the defendant's level of knowledge of computers and computer technology?

– What evidence exists showing the defendant is responsible for placing the images on the computer or media?

■ Video images may more clearly establish the elements of the offense.

■ Do the selected images adequately portray the offense charged? (For example, do the images graphically depict a sex act or merely suggest a sex act?)

■ Are faces visible?

■ Are the number and nature of the images selected adequate to counter the possible defense relating to the elements of the crime? (For example, it is more difficult to claim that 100 images were altered than to claim that 10 images were altered. Another consideration might be whether the same child is depicted in a number of different images.)

NOTE: Special considerations affect grand jury practice. Local practice may vary, but case law suggests the best course is to display rather than describe images to the grand jury. Any variation between images (or descriptions of images) that are presented before the grand jury and at trial may be fatal to the case.

III. Considerations: Jury selection

Because the charges and the evidence in a child pornography case can be subject to widely differing views, the jury selection process is crucial. Some prospective jurors may perceive child pornography as culturally acceptable or as a victimless crime. Additionally, many prospective jurors may not be able to understand computer technology and forensic evidence. Exploring attitudes regarding speech, computers, the Internet, and Federal, State, or local government regulations should identify jurors who are able to rely on digital evidence. Finally, questioning should discern whether jurors are prepared for what they will be exposed to in a child pornography case.

IV. Considerations: Trial

In trying child pornography cases, the prosecutor should consider how the court will control the evidence being viewed by and published to the jury, in addition to other persons in open court:

- Are the images printed out individually or otherwise?

- Is there a copy for each juror in addition to the copies for the judge and the reporter?

- Are the images displayed to the jury via computer and projector?

- Are appropriate controls in place concerning showing the evidence in open court such that it is or is not visible to the gallery?

- How will the images be preserved for appellate review?

These considerations may include format and size of images when shown as well as the manner in which they are handled in the jury room. The prosecutor should also consider the possible relevance of the original or native size of the image.

In the aftermath of the United States Supreme Court decision in *Ashcroft* v. *Free Speech Coalition,* 122 S. Ct. 1389 (2002) (holding that the Federal statutory prohibition involving sexually explicit images of children can constitutionally be applied only against images depicting "real" children), most courts have responded to the *Ashcroft* opinion by characterizing the issue simply as a factual question for the trier of fact to be decided on viewing the images. However, a few courts require the prosecution to present affirmative evidence in addition to the images themselves that the children depicted in the images are real as opposed to generated by computer. If evidence on this point is required, possible witnesses might include trained investigators, medical personnel, digital-imaging technicians, or investigators who can testify to the actual identity of the child in the image (from a "known" series) or who can testify to the image being in existence prior to the advent of digital imagery technology.

> NOTE: Many in this field anticipate that at some point in the future, distinguishing between images of real children and images of children that are entirely computer generated may be a significant evidentiary hurdle.

Courts also vary as to how age of the child must be proved. Most courts characterize the issue simply as a factual question for the trier of fact to decide based on the images. However, a few courts require the prosecution to present affirmative evidence concerning the age of the children depicted, in addition to the images themselves. If a court requires specific evidence on age, experienced or trained medical personnel may be used (e.g., a pediatrician or pediatric nurse).

V. Unanimity

Unanimity requirements vary according to local practice. If multiple images form the basis of a single count, it may be necessary in a jury trial to provide special verdict forms or otherwise ensure that the jurors unanimously decide which images violate the statute, and clearly identify these images in their verdict.

VI. Considerations: Discovery by the defense

Because child pornography is contraband, proper control, handling, and access restrictions should be considered at all times. The use of judicial protective orders or stipulations during the defense's discovery process is strongly advised. When the case has concluded, procedures should be in place for the return of the contraband to the prosecution for digital wiping or destruction.

Appendix A. Resources and Links

In addition to the other reports in its series on crime scene investigation and digital evidence (see Foreword), NIJ is releasing two multimedia companion products:

Using and Presenting Digital Evidence in the Courtroom, Digital Evidence Mock Trial

- Instructional Material in CD-ROM format, NCJ 215093, forthcoming Winter 2007.

- Mock Trial in DVD format, NCJ 215094, forthcoming Winter 2007.

Web sites

National Institute of Justice Electronic Crime Program, *www.ojp.usdoj.gov/nij/ topics/ecrime/welcome.html.* NIJ's Electronic Crime Program includes the Electronic Crime Partnership Initiative, the CyberScience Laboratory, the National Forensic Software Library, and Computer Forensic Tool Testing technical assistance resources.

U.S. Department of Justice, Computer Crime and Intellectual Property Section, *www.cybercrime.gov.* The site includes information on computer crime and intellectual property policy, cases, laws, and statutes and the guide *Searching and Seizing Computers and Obtaining Electronic Evidence in Criminal Investigations.*

National Advocacy Center (NAC), *www.usdoj.gov/usao/eousa/ole.* Operated by the U.S. Department of Justice, Executive Office for United States Attorneys, NAC trains Federal, State, and local prosecutors and litigators. The site provides information on available training classes, including computer forensics, Internet fraud, and cybercrime basics.

Federal Law Enforcement Training Center (FLETC), *www.fletc.gov.* FLETC, an agency of the U.S. Department of Homeland Security, provides specialized training for Federal, State, local, and international law enforcement officers. FLETC's Web site includes information on its available training classes on a range of subjects related to computer crime.

Department of Defense (DoD) Cyber Crime Center (DC3), *www.dc3.mil/dc3/ home.htm.* DC3 has three main programs: Defense Computer Forensics Laboratory, Defense Cyber Investigations Training Academy, and Defense Cyber Crime Institute. Each program provides critical training and forensic support to DoD personnel who analyze computer crime and electronic evidence.

National Association of Attorneys General (NAAG), *www.naag.org.* NAAG's site contains general information as well as its Computer Crime Point-of-Contact List of prosecutors and investigators from State and local law enforcement agencies in the United States who are responsible for investigating and prosecuting computer and computer-related crime in their respective jurisdictions.

National White Collar Crime Center (NW3C), *www.nw3c.org.* NW3C, a federally funded, nonprofit corporation, provides a nationwide support system for agencies involved in the prevention, investigation, and prosecution of economic and high-technology crimes. The site includes access to resources for training and research publications.

Forensic Association of Computer Technologists (F.A.C.T.), *www.comp4n6.org.* F.A.C.T. is a not-for-profit association that trains law enforcement personnel in the scientific techniques of examining computers. The Web site provides information on training opportunities (paid membership is required).

High Tech Crime Consortium, *www.hightechcrimecops.org.* The consortium offers investigators high-technology crime investigation education and training and expert consultants and develops software tools and techniques. The site has information on training offered and a quick reference to State statutes.

High Technology Crime Investigation Association (HTCIA), *www.htcia.org.* HTCIA encourages, promotes, and supports the voluntary interchange of information, experience, ideas, and knowledge among its members about methods, processes, and techniques relating to investigations of and security for advanced technologies. The site includes information on regional training opportunities (paid membership is required).

International Association of Computer Investigative Specialists (IACIS), *www.iacis.info/iacisv2/pages/home.php.* IACIS provides members access to newsletters, file libraries, and list servers for continuous communication and information sharing regarding digital forensics, technology advancements, and computer crimes.

Los Alamos National Laboratory (LANL), *www.lanl.gov.* LANL sponsors an annual conference on computer crime, including digital forensics for law enforcement. See www.lanl.gov for more information.

Peace Officer Standards and Training (POST). POST resources vary by State; many offer training and assistance regarding the handling of digital evidence.

SEARCH: The National Consortium for Justice Information and Statistics, *www.search.org.* This nonprofit membership organization is dedicated to improving the criminal justice system through better information management, effective application of information and identification technology, and responsible law and policy. Its Web site provides information on cybercrime training opportunities and technical assistance to criminal justice agencies.

E-mail newsletters

High Tech Crime Consortium investigator listserv, *www.hightechcrimecops.org/ joinhtcc.htm.* Restricted to law enforcement personnel, prosecutors, and corporate investigators tasked with investigating and prosecuting high-technology crime.

High Technology Crime Investigation Association, *www.htcia.org.* Paid membership is required.

International Association of Computer Investigative Specialists, *www.iacis.info/ iacisv2/pages/rules.php.* Paid membership is required.

Resources for network forensics

Casey, Eoghan, ed., *Handbook of Computer Crime Investigation: Forensic Tools and Technology,* San Diego: Academic Press, 2001.

Kruse, Warren G., II, and Jay G. Heiser, *Computer Forensics: Incident Response Essentials,* Boston: Addison-Wesley, 2001.

Mandia, Kevin, and Chris Prosise, *Incident Response: Investigating Computer Crime,* 2d ed., Berkeley, CA: McGraw-Hill, 2001.

Smith, Fred C., and Rebecca Gurley Bace, *A Guide to Forensic Testimony: The Art and Practice of Presenting Testimony as an Expert Technical Witness,* Boston: Addison-Wesley, 2002.

Stephenson, Peter, *Investigating Computer-Related Crime,* Boca Raton, FL: CRC Press, 1999.

Resources for courtroom preparation and evidence rules

Fenwick, William A., and G.K. Davidson, "Admissibility of Computerized Business Records," *American Jurisprudence Proof of Facts,* 2d ed., 14(1977)(2000 supp.): 173–251.

Kurzban, Stanley A., "Authentication of Computer-Generated Evidence in the United States Federal Courts," *IDEA: The Journal of Law and Technology* 35(4)(1995): 437–461.

Miller, Robin Cheryl, "Validity of Search or Seizure of Computer, Computer Disk, or Computer Peripheral Equipment," *American Law Reports* 84(5th)1(2001).

Scott, Michael D., *Internet and Technology Law Desk Reference,* Gaithersburg, MD: Aspen Law and Business, 1999.

Zupanec, Donald M., "Admissibility of Computerized Business Records," *American Law Reports* 7(4th)8(1981, 2000 Supp.).

Appendix B. Electronic Communications Privacy Act Disclosure Rules

	Voluntary disclosure allowed?		Mechanisms to compel disclosure	
	Public provider	**Nonpublic provider**	**Public provider**	**Nonpublic provider**
Basic subscriber, session, and billing information	Not to government unless § 2702(c) exception applies [§2702(a)(3)]	Yes [§2702(a)(3)]	Subpoena, 2703(d) order or search warrant [§2703(c)(2)]	Subpoena, 2703(d) order or search warrant [§2703(c)(2)]
Other transactional and account records	Not to government unless §2702(c) exception applies [§2702(a)(3)]	Yes [§2702(a)(3)]	2703(d) order or search warrant [§2703(c)(1)]	2703(d) order or search warrant [§2703(c)(1)]
Accessed communications (opened e-mail and voice mail) left with provider and other stored files	No, unless §2702(b) exception applies [§2702(a)(2)]	Yes [§2702(a)(2)]	Subpoena with notice, 2703(d) order with notice, or search warrant [§2703(b)]	Subpoena; ECPA does not apply [§2711(2)]
Unretrieved communication, including e-mail and voice mail (in electronic storage more than 180 days)	No, unless §2702(b) exception applies [§2702(a)(1)]	Yes [§2702(a)(1)]	Subpoena with notice, 2703(d) order with notice, or search warrant [§2703(a, b)]	Subpoena with notice, 2703(d) order with notice, or search warrant [§2703(a, b)]
Unretrieved communication, including e-mail and voice mail (in electronic storage 180 days or fewer)	No, unless §2702(b) exception applies [§2702(a)(1)]	Yes [§2702(a)(1)]	Search warrant [§2703(a)]	Search warrant [§2703(a)]

Note: Judicial interpretations of these provisions may vary.

Appendix C. Sample Consent Forms

Sample 1: Consent to Search

(Adapted from Maine Computer Crimes Task Force Consent-to-Search Form)

I hereby give my consent and permission for the items described below to be searched by law enforcement officer _____, and by any law enforcement officer of the _____ [*insert name of task force or agency*].

I hereby state that I myself have the authority and the ability to gain access to, possess, inspect, examine, and search the items described below.

I understand that I have the right to refuse to give my consent to search the items described below. I give my consent to this search voluntarily and as an act of my own free will, and not because of any threats, compulsion, promises, or inducements. I further state that no threats or promises have been made to compel or induce me to sign this consent form.

I understand that any items, images, documents, or other evidence discovered pursuant to a search of the items described below may be used as evidence in a court of law.

Items to be searched (description, serial numbers, etc.): _____

_____

_____

_____

_____

_____

_____

_____

By signing this form, I hereby declare that I have read and understood its contents entirely.

_____   _____
Signature   Date

Witnessed by:

_____   _____
Witness/Law Enforcement Officer   Date

Sample 2: Consent to Search

I, _____, hereby consent to search of the following locations, vehicles, and articles by Agents of _____ *[insert name of task force or agency]* or other local, State, or Federal law enforcement personnel.

Home/Business Address(s)

1.) _____   2.) _____

    _____   _____

    _____   _____

This consent extends to any and all yards, garages, carports, outbuildings, storage areas, sheds, trash containers, or mailboxes assigned to the above listed premises.

_____
Initials

Vehicle(s)

Make/Model _____

Year/License _____

Make/Model _____

Year/License _____

I understand that this consent includes authorization to remove all computers, hard drives, and other electronic storage media (CDs, DVDs, floppy discs, Zip® discs, Jaz® cartridges, Smart Media Cards, Compact Flash, Memory Sticks, etc.) for examination offsite at a secure facility using appropriate tools and techniques.

_____
Initials

This consent is freely and voluntarily given. I have not been coerced or threatened, nor have any promises been made regarding my cooperation in this investigation.

_____   _____

Signature   Date

_____   _____

Witness/Law Enforcement Officer   Date

Sample 3: Supplemental Consent to Search

To assist agents of the _____ *[insert name of task force or agency]*, or other local, State, or Federal law enforcement personnel with their search of computers, hard drives, and other electronic storage media seized with my consent, I am providing the following information:

Screen Saver/BIOS Password

| |
| |
| |

Other Passwords/Usernames

Program/Service	Username	Password

Encryption Keys

Public Key	Private Key

Initials

Sample 4: Supplemental Consent to Search (Internet Service Provider/Web-Based E-Mail)

I, _____, hereby consent to agents of _____ *[insert name of task force or agency]*, or other local, State, or Federal law enforcement personnel who are accessing, viewing, downloading, printing, and/or copying the contents of any electronic mail in all folders (sent, received, trash, etc.) stored offsite by my Internet service provider or Web based e-mail provider. In cooperation with this search, I am freely and voluntarily providing the following account names, user names, and passwords:

Internet Service Provider (e.g., AOL, Yahoo, Hotmail, etc.)	Username	Password

This consent is limited to a one-time only access for purposes of viewing, downloading, copying, and/or printing and expires 48 hours after the listed date and time.

_____   _____   _____
Signature   Date   Time

_____   _____   _____
Witness/Law Enforcement Officer   Date   Time

Appendix D. Stipulation Regarding Evidence Returned to the Defendant

_____, in the interest of expediting the searching and seizing of
   [Suspect]

records and other evidence as authorized by Search Warrant #_____, signed by

_____, Judge, on _____, so as to minimize interruption of the
                                        [date]

normal computing activities of _____, stipulate to the
                                  [suspect or suspect's company]

following terms applicable to the records, equipment, and evidence itemized in the

attached inventory, incorporated by reference:

_____, is satisfied that the backup or forensic copies made
   [Suspect]

on _____, are complete and accurate copies of the entire contents of the sys-
    [date]

tems searched as of that date. _____, will not contest the
                                        [Suspect]

accuracy, reliability, or source of any record copied, printed out, or derived from

those backups/forensic copies. _____ waives any objection
                                        [Suspect]

as to best evidence, authenticity, or foundation as to any record copied, printed out,

or derived from those backups/forensic copies.

Appendix E. Glossary

Agent: A person who serves the interests of an agency that has jurisdiction over criminal or civil matters involving digital evidence. In many jurisdictions and circumstances, the agent will be a law enforcement officer. However, an agent may also be a nonsworn individual of suitable qualification who is serving the interests of the parties involved in a criminal or civil investigation or dispute.

Buddy list: A collection of screen names, usually compiled by a user for "instant messaging" on his or her personal computer or cellular telephone.

Copy (v.): Accurately reproduce information contained on an original physical item, independent of the electronic storage device (e.g., logical file copy). Maintains contents, but attributes may change during the reproduction.

Digital evidence: Information stored or transmitted in binary form that may be relied on in court.

Documentation: Written notes, audiotapes, videotapes, printed forms, sketches, and photographs that form a detailed record of the scene, evidence recovered, and actions taken during the search of the scene.

Duplicate: An accurate digital reproduction of all data contained on a digital storage device (e.g., hard drive, CD-ROM, flash memory, floppy disk, Zip®, Jaz®). Maintains contents and attributes (e.g., bit stream, bit copy, and sector dump).

Duplicate digital evidence: An accurate digital reproduction of all data objects contained on the original physical item.

ECPA: In this guide, refers to the stored communications chapter of the Electronic Communications Privacy Act, 18 U.S.C. § 2701 et seq.

Electronic device: A device that operates on principles governing the behavior of electrons.

Electronic evidence: Information and data of investigative value that are stored in or transmitted by an electronic device.

Encryption: Any procedure used in cryptography to convert plain text into cipher-text so as to prevent anyone but the intended recipient from reading the data.

First responder: The initial responding law enforcement officer(s) and/or other public safety official(s) arriving at the scene.

FRE: Federal Rules of Evidence.

High-technology crime: Criminal offenses that involve computer technology, including computer crimes, computer-related crimes, and Internet-related crimes.

ISP: Internet service provider. ISPs are organizations that provide subscribers with access to the Internet. Small ISPs provide service via modem and ISDN (Integrated Services Digital Network), while the larger ones also offer private line hookups (e.g., T1, fractional T1).

Metadata: Data about data.

Network: A group of computers connected to one another to share information and resources.

Server: A computer that provides some service for other computers that are connected to it via a network.

Sniffer: Software that monitors network packets and can be used to intercept data including passwords, credit card numbers, etc.

Special master: Court-appointed independent person in a quasi-judicial role who assists a judge by deciding, in cases that involve files, data, or other evidence that may be protected by an evidentiary or testimonial privilege, which of the files, data, or other evidence are indeed protected by a privilege (hence, *not* to be released to investigators) and those that are not protected (releasable to investigators).

Taint team (or privilege team): Government investigators and attorneys who are involved in a case solely to work with the defense to determine, prior to release to the case investigation or prosecution team, whether or not files, data, or other evidence are protected by an evidentiary or testimonial privilege. In the event a claim of privilege is raised by the defense but is disputed, the taint team and the defense are able to bring the matter before the court in a confidential manner without members of the investigation or prosecution team present. Members of a taint team are isolated from the case investigation and prosecution team by an "ethical wall" and are not permitted to discuss their work except with the court.

Trier of fact: The person or persons who decide the facts in legal cases. In a jury trial the jury is the trier of fact. When there is no jury (sometimes called a "bench trial" or "trial to the court"), the judge is the trier of fact. With or without a jury, it is the judge who determines the law in a case.

URL: Universal Resource Locator.

About the National Institute of Justice

NIJ is the research, development, and evaluation agency of the U.S. Department of Justice. NIJ's mission is to advance scientific research, development, and evaluation to enhance the administration of justice and public safety. NIJ's principal authorities are derived from the Omnibus Crime Control and Safe Streets Act of 1968, as amended (see 42 U.S.C. §§ 3721–3723).

The NIJ Director is appointed by the President and confirmed by the Senate. The Director establishes the Institute's objectives, guided by the priorities of the Office of Justice Programs, the U.S. Department of Justice, and the needs of the field. The Institute actively solicits the views of criminal justice and other professionals and researchers to inform its search for the knowledge and tools to guide policy and practice.

Strategic Goals

NIJ has seven strategic goals grouped into three categories:

Creating relevant knowledge and tools

1. Partner with State and local practitioners and policymakers to identify social science research and technology needs.
2. Create scientific, relevant, and reliable knowledge—with a particular emphasis on terrorism, violent crime, drugs and crime, cost-effectiveness, and community-based efforts—to enhance the administration of justice and public safety.
3. Develop affordable and effective tools and technologies to enhance the administration of justice and public safety.

Dissemination

4. Disseminate relevant knowledge and information to practitioners and policymakers in an understandable, timely, and concise manner.
5. Act as an honest broker to identify the information, tools, and technologies that respond to the needs of stakeholders.

Agency management

6. Practice fairness and openness in the research and development process.
7. Ensure professionalism, excellence, accountability, cost-effectiveness, and integrity in the management and conduct of NIJ activities and programs.

Program Areas

In addressing these strategic challenges, the Institute is involved in the following program areas: crime control and prevention, including policing; drugs and crime; justice systems and offender behavior, including corrections; violence and victimization; communications and information technologies; critical incident response; investigative and forensic sciences, including DNA; less-than-lethal technologies; officer protection; education and training technologies; testing and standards; technology assistance to law enforcement and corrections agencies; field testing of promising programs; and international crime control.

In addition to sponsoring research and development and technology assistance, NIJ evaluates programs, policies, and technologies. NIJ communicates its research and evaluation findings through conferences and print and electronic media.

To find out more about the National Institute of Justice, please visit:

http://www.ojp.usdoj.gov/nij

or contact:

National Criminal Justice
 Reference Service
P.O. Box 6000
Rockville, MD 20849–6000
800–851–3420
e-mail: *askncjrs@ncjrs.org*